IN THE STRENGTH OF HIS MIGHT

Remaining Faithful in the Great Tribulation

SUSAN E. JEANS

In the Strength of His Might

Print ISBN 978-1-941512-00-5
Ebook ISBN 978-1-941512-32-6

Copyright © 2014 by Susan E. Jeans

Published by
    Master Design Publishing
    789 State Route 94 E
    Fulton, KY 42041
    www.MasterDesign.org

Scripture quotations taken from the New American Standard Bible®, Copyright © 1960, 1962, 1963, 1968, 1971, 1972, 1973, 1975, 1977, 1995 by The Lockman Foundation. Used by permission. (www.Lockman.org)

All rights reserved. No part of this publication may be reproduced, stored in a retrieval system or transmitted in any way by any means, electronic, mechanical, photocopy, recording or otherwise, without the prior permission of the author, except as provided by USA and international copyright law.

Cover design by Mila Perry and Faithe Thomas.

Printed in the USA.   JJ

For my daughters

Contents

Preface 1
Chapter 1: What is the tribulation period? 5
    A. Israel's place in God's plan 5
    B. Daniel's 70 weeks 6
    C. A seven-year "week" 10
    D. The gap between the first 69 weeks and the 70th week 12
    E. Summary of Daniel 9:24-27 16
    F. Jesus' teaching about the Great Tribulation within the 70th week 18
    G. Biblical names for the 70th week 20
Chapter 2: Is the Great Tribulation relevant to Christians? 23
    A. Setting the stage in Revelation: the scroll with seven seals 23
    B. The parallels between Revelation 6 and Matthew 24 25
        1. The first seal: the antichrist 26
        2. The second seal: war 28
        3. The third seal: famine 28
        4. The fourth seal: death and hades 29
        5. The fifth seal: martyrs under the altar 33
        6. The sixth seal: cataclysmic upheavals in the heavens and on earth . 37
    C. The relationship between the 70th week and
          God's wrath in the Day of the Lord 38
    D. The presence of Christians on earth during the Great Tribulation 44
Chapter 3: Who is the antichrist? 47
    A. Origin of the term "antichrist" 47
    B. Revelations from Daniel 2 and 7 48
    C. The beasts of Revelation 13 and 17 51

 D. The past beast kings and kingdoms represented by the seven heads of the beast 53

 E. The eighth king (the antichrist) and his empire .58

 F. Further insights from Daniel 11:36 and following. 62

 G. Clues to the origin or ethnicity of the antichrist from Daniel 9:26. 68

 H. Forerunner/prototype in Antiochus Epiphanes. 72

 I. The end of the antichrist 77

Chapter 4: What is the rapture and when is it?. 79

 A. Biblical descriptions of the rapture. 79

 B. Spiritual bodies. 81

 C. Connection of the rapture to the Day of the Lord 83

  1. Deliverance of the just immediately before delivery of judgment . . .83

  2. Timing of both the rapture and the Day of the Lord. 90

   (a) After the apostasy 90

   (b) After the revelation of the man of lawlessness. 92

   (c) After the Great Tribulation 93

Chapter 5: How do Christians prepare for the Great Tribulation?. 97

 A. Submission to the Lordship of Jesus Christ. 97

  1. Why people need a Savior, a Redeemer 98

  2. The double transfer 100

 B. Growing relationship with Jesus Christ 102

 C. Avoiding deception 106

 D. Remaining faithful in "the strength of His might" 111

Afterword 115

Appendix. 117

 Biblical Descriptions of the Antichrist 117

 The Sequence of Events Within Daniel's 70th Week 122

Preface

Why should there be yet another book printed on the subject of the Second Coming of Christ, the end times, the Great Tribulation, or the rapture? Is there not already a glut of such books on the market? The answer to these questions is that the subject of this book is quite limited in scope. It is addressed to people who characterize themselves as Christian, but who are not particularly well-versed (pun intended!) on the prophetic portions of the Bible. It is also addressed to those who are somewhat familiar with Biblical prophecies regarding the end of the last days, but who believe that they need not concern themselves with studying those prophecies, either: (1) because they believe the fulfillment is far in the future, past their lifetimes; or (2) because they believe the prophecies do not apply to them.

Recently, I have been pressed with a terrible sense of urgency to sound the alarm to anyone who will listen: (1) that the time of the fulfillment of these prophecies is drawing very near; and (2) that we need to be prepared for the fulfillment of these prophecies because they *will* apply, in one way or another, to everyone. In particular, this book is focused on the warnings that Jesus gave in Matthew 24:4-27, warnings which have their parallel in the first six seals of Revelation chapter 6.

Some Christians believe that all the warnings that Jesus gave in the Olivet Discourse (Matthew 24 and 25) and in the Revelation to John some 60 years later, were and are only for the Jews, because the recipients of this teaching by Jesus were Jewish believers, called disciples. But Jewish believers were the first Christians. Through those first Jewish Christians, Jesus was, by extension, talking to all believers, whether Jewish or Gentile. Of course, some of His warnings would apply only to those in and around Jerusalem, but, like the command to observe the Last Supper, and like the command to spread the gospel to the entire world, both of which were given just to these same Jewish disciples, the message is for all believers living at the appointed time.

I would very much like to side with those Christians who believe that we Christians will not be here on earth during the terrible time of the Great Tribulation; after all, that is what *I* was taught when I first became a Christian. But in subsequent years, I have come to the conclusion that the seals of Revelation chapter 6 are not the wrath of God and, therefore, Christians *will* be around during the Great Tribulation. Moreover, the virtual explosion of technology, the evaporation of personal privacy, the increasing intrusion of government into the personal lives of citizens, and the eradication of Christianity and our Judeo-Christian roots from the American culture, are all changing the character of the prophecies of Revelation from science fiction to scientific realities. All Americans, but especially those who call themselves Christian, need to shake off the spiritual lethargy and lukewarmness we have slipped into as a result of our indulgent lives of luxury; we need to wake up to the realities around us, and get serious about getting firmly grounded and rooted in the faith "which was once for all delivered to the saints" (Jude 3), so that, when the hurricane winds of the Great Tribulation blow, we will be able to stand firm. But in times of trial, especially in the unprecedented Great Tribulation, *how* can we stand firm? The answer is in the title of this book, **"in the strength of His might."** The phrase comes from Ephesians 1:18 and 6:10, which are cited in their respective contexts below.

I cannot know in which generation these prophesied events will occur; but I think it is best to use the time we have now – while we still have access to our Bibles, and while we are still allowed to meet freely for Bible study – to prepare as if we *will* be here during those tumultuous times. Then, if the Great Tribulation should occur during our lifetimes, and if we are still here on earth, we will have heeded the Lord's warnings and we will not be *deceived*.

Susan E. Jeans
December 31, 2013

Ephesians 1:15-23

¹⁵*For this reason I too, having heard of the faith in the Lord Jesus which exists among you, and your love for all the saints,* ¹⁶*do not cease giving thanks for you, while making mention of you in my prayers;* ¹⁷*that the God of our Lord Jesus Christ, the Father of glory, may give to you a spirit of wisdom and of revelation in the knowledge of Him.* ¹⁸*I pray that the eyes of your heart may be enlightened, so that you may know what is the hope of His calling, what are the riches of the glory of His inheritance in the saints,* ¹⁹*and what is the surpassing greatness of His power toward us who believe. These are in accordance with the working of* **the strength of His might** ²⁰*which He brought about in Christ, when He raised Him from the dead, and seated Him at His right hand in the heavenly places,* ²¹*far above all rule and authority and power and dominion, and every name that is named, not only in this age, but also in the one to come.* ²²*And He put all things in subjection under His feet, and gave Him as head over all things to the Church,* ²³*which is His body, the fulness of Him who fills all in all.*

Ephesians 6:10-17

¹⁰*Finally, be strong in the Lord, and* **in the strength of His might.** ¹¹*Put on the full armor of God, that you may be able to stand firm against the schemes of the devil.* ¹²*For our struggle is not against flesh and blood, but against the rulers, against the powers, against the world forces of this darkness, against the spiritual forces of wickedness in the heavenly places.* ¹³*Therefore, take up the full armor of God, that you may be able to resist in the evil day, and having done everything, to stand firm.* ¹⁴*Stand firm therefore, having girded your loins with truth, and having put on the breastplate of righteousness,* ¹⁵*and having shod your feet with the preparation of the gospel of peace;* ¹⁶*in addition to all, taking up the shield of faith with which you will be able to extinguish all the flaming missiles of the evil one.* ¹⁷*And*

take the helmet of salvation, and the sword of the Spirit, which is the word of God.

For clarity of communication, a timeline chart is printed on the inside back cover and a few definitions of Biblical terms are printed on the inside of the front cover.

• 1 •

What is the Tribulation Period?

A. Israel's place in God's plan

If you are looking for information in the Bible about the end times, it seems that the logical place to start would be the last book of the Bible, Revelation. If you search the text of Revelation for words and phrases like "the end times," "the last days," and "the Great Tribulation," however, you will not find them there. Then where do these concepts come from? The answer is: from other books in the Bible. Most of the Old Testament prophets wrote about the final days of human history on this present earth, and several New Testament writers added more information.

In order to understand the future events that are set out in Revelation, it is necessary to begin with the present time, and then take a quick look backward. If you follow the news, you will have noticed that a great deal of time and newsprint are taken up with the volatile Middle East. All of it seems to center on the controversy over possession of the land of Israel. The Jews as a people and a nation date back to the time of Abraham, 4,000 years ago. No other people group, no other nation, dispersed from their land, has survived nearly as long. The continued existence of the Jews as a distinct people group throughout the vast majority of human history, despite all the best efforts of various nations and individuals to annihilate them, is an astonishing fact that has caused many to wonder about the secret of their survival.

The answer is that God sovereignly chose this nation out of all the peoples of the world to be His representative on earth, and from this people group would arise the Messiah. Jesus told the Samaritan woman at the well, in John 4:22, that salvation is from the Jews. Some translations say, "salvation is *of* the Jews." And the miracle of the preservation of the Jews as a distinct nation throughout history, despite the fact that the Jews were dispersed among the nations twice and expelled from their land from A.D. 70 to 1948, is, as it always was, attributable to the sovereign hand of God. Any other people group would have been assimilated and absorbed into the nations of the world. The only explanation for the fact that the Jews still exist as a distinct people is that God is not finished with them yet. *That* is the secret of the survival of the Jews.

But what is the role of Israel in God's eternal plan? Was it completed with the coming of the Messiah? The answer is no, and found within the explanation of the answer is the time frame of Revelation, including that of the Great Tribulation. It is in the Old Testament book of Daniel that the concept of the "70th week," the last seven years of this present age, is revealed.

B. Daniel's 70 weeks

The concept of "70 weeks" originates in chapter 9 of Daniel. The primary goal in examining Daniel chapter 9 is to lay a foundation for understanding two things: (1) God's as-yet-unfinished plan for Israel; and (2) the time frame for the book of Revelation.

The main theme of the book of Daniel is that God is sovereign over all the history of all the nations of mankind. It was God who punished the southern kingdom of Israel, which was known as Judah, by allowing Nebuchadnezzar, the Babylonian king, to conquer God's people. Through His prophets, God had repeatedly warned His people to turn away from their idolatry, worship Him alone, and obey His law.

There was a particular command in the Law that had not been obeyed; it was in Leviticus chapter 25, which Daniel would have been taught as a child. For six years the people were to work the land, but during the seventh year, the land was to have a Sabbath rest. God had warned His people *in advance* that, if they would not let the land rest every seventh year, He Himself would give the land all its accumulated Sabbath rests by taking the people out of the land until the land had been given all those Sabbath rests. This is recorded in Leviticus 26:33-35. But, because God's people did not trust Him to provide a bumper crop for them each sixth year so that they would have enough to eat during the seventh year while the land was having its Sabbath rest, they never stopped planting and harvesting.

In addition to warning His people of the consequences of failure to observe His Law, the Lord, through His prophets, foretold exactly *how* He would give the land its Sabbath rests. One of those prophets was Jeremiah, who was a contemporary of Daniel, although he was older. Jeremiah's ministry was about half over when Daniel's began. In Jeremiah 20 and 25, the Lord told His people in Judah that He was going to punish them by bringing the barbaric Babylonians to conquer them and to take them into captivity for 70 years. During that time period that the people were removed out of the land, the land would be given its accumulated Sabbath rests; but when the 70 years were completed, then He would punish the Babylonians by using the Persians and the Medes to conquer them, and the Israelites would be allowed to return to their land.

The historical account of the fall of Judah to the Babylonians is recorded not only very briefly in Daniel chapter 1 but also in greater detail in II Chronicles 36:14-21. Verse 18 of II Chronicles 36 says: "All the articles of the house of God" – that means Solomon's Temple – "and the treasures of the house of the Lord, he" – meaning Nebuchadnezzar – "brought them all to Babylon." Verse 19 says: "Then they burned the house of God, and broke down the wall of Jerusalem and burned all its fortified buildings with fire."

Daniel was a member of either the royal family or of the nobility of Judah, and he was taken into captivity by the Babylonians when he was a young teenager. He spent the remainder of his life in Babylon and never returned home. Nevertheless, he had in his possession the writings of Jeremiah. Chapter 9 of the book of Daniel takes place when Daniel had been in captivity for approximately 67 years. As he studied the prophecies of Jeremiah, he took the 70 years literally, and realized that the time of captivity was almost completed. While the captivity had been punitive in nature, its ultimate purpose was restoration of relationship. God was disciplining His people to break them of their idolatry, to push them to repent and to return to a proper relationship with Him, and to obey His law as a demonstration of their fidelity to Him.

Having lived for most of his life with the exiles in Babylon, Daniel knew that the chastening rod of God had not accomplished its intended purpose. The people had not repented and returned to the worship of God. But Daniel also knew that God would keep *His* promises, and He had promised to return the people to their land after a period of 70 years. So, after a period of extensive preparation, Daniel began to entreat God, and a portion of his eloquent prayer is recorded as chapter 9 of the book of Daniel. Daniel begged God to forgive and to restore the people of Israel, not only because it would be an act of mercy, but also because it would bring honor and glory to God, as His city and His people were called by His name.

Although the full length of Daniel's prayer is unknown, by the time of the evening sacrifice, he had become extremely weary. At that time, the angel Gabriel appeared to him to give him "insight with understanding" in response to his petition. Gabriel explained two things to Daniel:

1. The desolations for Israel and the Temple would not end with the completion of the 70 years of captivity.

2. Israel's sin was not over because she had not repented and returned to the Lord.

Therefore, because Israel had not responded to God's judgment of the 70-year captivity, He would multiply the years of punishment seven times. This was foretold in that same chapter 26 of Leviticus. In verse 18, God warned: "If also after these things" – meaning, in this context, the Babylonian captivity – "you do not obey Me, then I will punish you seven times more for your sins."

The enigmatic last four verses of Daniel 9 are God's enactment of the sevenfold punishment of Leviticus 26:18. If 70 years of punishment for the broken Sabbath years would not elicit the appropriate response from Israel, then God would keep His word and extend the period sevenfold. These last four verses of Daniel chapter 9 contain one of the most important prophecies of the Old Testament. In these verses, Gabriel reveals to Daniel *God's purposes for Israel*:

Daniel 9

[24]"Seventy weeks have been decreed for your people and your holy city, to finish the transgression, to make an end of sin, to make atonement for iniquity, to bring in everlasting righteousness, to seal up vision and prophecy, and to anoint the most holy place. [25]"So you are to know and discern that from the issuing of a decree to restore and rebuild Jerusalem until Messiah the Prince there will be seven weeks and sixty-two weeks; it will be built again, with plaza and moat, even in times of distress. [26]"Then after the sixty-two weeks the Messiah will be cut off and have nothing, and the people of the prince who is to come will destroy the city and the sanctuary. And its end will come with a flood; even to the end there will be war; desolations are determined. [27]"And he will make a firm covenant with the many for one week, but in the middle of the week he will put a stop to sacrifice and grain offering; and on the wing of abominations will come one who makes desolate, even until a complete destruction, one that is decreed, is poured out on the one who makes desolate."

This passage is hardly self-explanatory! Let's work our way through it.

C. A seven-year "week"

The Hebrew word that is translated into the English word "weeks" is shabuwa (transliterated) and it literally means "sevened." Thus, it is translated as "seven," meaning a period of seven. Because the prophecies of the first 69 of those periods of seven were fulfilled in 483 *years*, it is clear that the period of seven cannot mean seven days or seven months, but rather must mean years.

Since the word translated into English as "seven" means a period of seven years, then 70 periods of seven years each would be 70 x 7, or 490 years. This makes sense because the Babylonian captivity was 70 literal years and it was being 'sevened' – multiplied by 7. Thus, Gabriel was telling Daniel about a time period of 490 years. Here is the overview of the divine message:

Verse 24: The prophecy as a whole is presented.
Verse 25: The first 69 sevens or weeks are described.
Verse 26: The events between the 69th seven and the 70th seven are detailed.
Verse 27: The final period of the 70th seven, or 70th week, is described.

Verse 24 is easier to see and to understand if it is set out structurally:
Seventy weeks have been decreed for your people
    and your holy city,
        to finish the transgression,
        to make an end of sin,
        to make atonement for iniquity,
        to bring in everlasting righteousness,
        to seal up vision and prophecy, and
        to anoint the most holy place.

Setting out the verse this way demonstrates plainly that, by the end of this period of 70 weeks, six things will have been accomplished. It is important to remember that Gabriel is speaking to Daniel about *his* people and *his* holy city. That means that this prophecy applies to the Jews and to Jerusalem. It is not a prophecy that applies to the Church, even though the Church is made up of Jews and Gentiles, nor does it apply to Gentiles, at least not directly.

Daniel 9:25 then describes the first 69 sevens or weeks: "So you are to know and discern that from the issuing of a decree to restore and rebuild Jerusalem until Messiah the Prince there will be seven weeks and sixty-two weeks; it will be built again, with plaza and moat, even in times of distress."

It is not clear why the first 69 weeks are broken down into seven weeks of 49 years and 62 weeks of 434 years, which are immediately consecutive. Nevertheless, 7 weeks + 62 weeks = 69 weeks. Since each week equals 7 years, then 7 x 69 = 483 years. According to verse 25, what denotes the beginning of this 483 years? The issuing of a decree to restore and rebuild Jerusalem. What denotes the end of this 483 years? The arrival of Messiah, Jesus Christ (what we know as His first coming).

This sounds relatively straightforward, but the problem is that there were several decrees relating to the return of the exiles. The decree that most scholars believe is the one that is intended does refer specifically to the rebuilding of the *city of Jerusalem*, rather than to the rebuilding of the Temple, or to simply returning, with no reference to rebuilding anything. Thus, the operative decree was apparently issued by Artaxerxes, about 90 years after the first captives returned and started the rebuilding of the Temple. This is recorded in Nehemiah 2:1-8. The year was approximately 445 B.C. This decree of Artaxerxes, allowing Nehemiah to return to Jerusalem to supervise the rebuilding of the city walls, seems to fit most closely with the description of rebuilding the plaza – some translations say "street" – and digging some sort of defensive moat and wall around the city to protect it from invaders. Nehemiah's own account confirms that the rebuilding took place in a time of trouble.

D. The gap between the first 69 weeks and the 70th week

The passage in Daniel 9:24-27 sets out four time periods.
1. A period of seven "weeks" of seven years each (49 years);

2. A period of 62 "weeks" of seven years each (434 years);

3. A gap of indeterminate length; and

4. A 70th "week" of seven years.

The first two periods, those of the seven weeks and the 62 weeks, for a total of 69 weeks, or 483 years, are described in Daniel 9:25 and have been fulfilled historically. That time period of 483 years ended with the first coming of the Messiah, Jesus Christ. This sets **the beginning of the gap**, which is described in Daniel 9:26. This verse describes two events: the crucifixion of the Messiah and the destruction of Jerusalem and the Temple. Both of those were fulfilled in history. Then Daniel 9:27 describes the beginning of the 70th week, which would also be **the end of the gap**.

Why do these verses require a gap between the 69th and 70th weeks?

1. Interruption of the sequence of events described in Daniel 9:26-27

The very language used in verses 26 and 27 indicates that something happens that interrupts the flow of the sequence of events. Verse 26 describes two events that occur after the end of the 7 + 62 weeks, meaning after the end of the 69th week. The first part of this verse 26 says: "Then **after** the sixty-two weeks the Messiah will be cut off and have nothing…" The "cutting off" of the Messiah is the first event listed in this verse. The next part of verse 26 reveals that, in addition to the "cutting off" of the Messiah, another event will occur: "… the people of the prince who is to come will destroy the city and the sanctuary.…"

Directly after this description of the second event in verse 26, which is the destruction of Jerusalem and the Temple, verse 27 speaks of sacrifices and grain offerings occurring once more in the Temple. It follows that, somewhere between verse 26 and 27, the Temple must be re-built. But from A.D. 70, when the destruction of the Temple described in verse 26 occurred, until now, 2014, there has been no Temple rebuilt. Therefore, Daniel's 70th week, which verse 27 describes, cannot have occurred yet. That is the first reason why there must be a gap between the 69th and 70th weeks.

2. Timing of the fulfillment of the events of verse 26

Verse 25 describes the events of the first 69 weeks, or 483 years, and they have been fulfilled. At least one of the events of verse 26 (the destruction of Jerusalem and the Temple) did not occur in the seven years following the end of the 69th week. History records that the destruction of Jerusalem occurred in A.D. 70, approximately *40 years after* the crucifixion of Christ. If the 70th week— a period of seven years— had followed immediately after the 69th week, the 70 weeks would have ended before the event prophesied (the destruction of Jerusalem and the Temple) had occurred. In other words, the events of verse 26 did not occur in the seven years after the 69th week; they occurred approximately 40 years after the end of the 69th week. This is a second reason why there must be a gap between the end of the 69th week and the onset of the 70th week.

3. Events of verse 27, the 70th week, still future

The last part of verse 26 says: "And its end will come with a flood; **even to the end** there will be war; desolations are determined."

"Desolations" depict a state of devastation or ruin or emptiness. This language indicates that the destruction of Jerusalem would be like the destruction of a flood, especially if it is viewed as a flood of wrath, and that desolations are sovereignly determined until the end. Beginning with the phrase "even to the end," there is a shift from past fulfillment to past, present, and future fulfillment. It seems that, even though the Jews returned to their land beginning in 1948, and have even had control of parts of Jerusalem since 1967, there has been no end of war, or the constant threat of war.

Like the prophecies of Daniel 9:25, most of the prophesied events of verse 26 have been fulfilled; the exception would be the constant threat of war "even to the end." Indeed, the prophecies of the first 69 weeks, or 483 years, have been fulfilled exactly as they were prophesied. In contrast, there has been no seven-year period in history fulfilling the events of verse 27— not in the seven-year period following the end of the 69th week and not in any time in the millennia since. This is a third reason why there must be a gap between the end of the 69th week and the onset of the 70th week.

Verse 27 describes the onset of, the activities during, and the end of, the 70th week: "And he will make a firm covenant with the many for one week, but in the middle of the week he will put a stop to sacrifice and grain offering; and on the wing of abominations will come one who makes desolate, even until a complete destruction, one that is decreed, is poured out on the one who makes desolate."

The verse begins with the pronoun "he." Who is "he?" "He" is the "prince who is to come" of verse 26. He will make a covenant with the many. "The many" is a reference to unbelieving Jews who will enter into an alliance with this prince who is to come. This conclusion is deduced from the fact that the beginning of the prophecy, verse 24, says that the whole prophecy of verses 24 through 27 concerns Daniel's people – the Jews; and Daniel's holy city – Jerusalem.

Since the first 69 weeks involved a literal 483-year period of time, this 70th week should also be a literal seven-year period. This final period of seven years, the 70th week, will begin with the introduction of a covenant relationship between a future "prince who is to come" and "the many," the people of Israel. The "prince who is to come" will be "the antichrist." The primary subject of the covenant will likely be some sort of peace treaty between Israel and her neighbors who despise her. In addition, the control and governance of the city of Jerusalem and the Temple mount will surely be addressed. It is probable that the covenant will also include the rebuilding of the Temple – this would be the third Temple – and the reinstitution of the Mosaic sacrificial system, if these have not already been accomplished before the signing of the covenant. In any event, the Mosaic sacrificial system will have to be back in operation prior to the midpoint of this 70th week, because Daniel 9:27, says that at the midpoint, he, the prince who is to come, will put a stop to the sacrifices – a clear reference to the Mosaic system of Temple sacrifices. Obviously, sacrifices cannot be stopped until the Temple is rebuilt in some form and the Mosaic sacrificial system is re-instituted.

Thus, according to Daniel 9:27, there are two things that will happen at the midpoint of the 70th week, that is, after 3½ years. The first is that the "prince who is come," the antichrist, will break the covenant by putting a stop to sacrifice and grain offering. But in addition to stopping the Mosaic sacrifices, the antichrist will desecrate the future Temple. This is described in the middle part of verse 27: "And he will make a firm covenant with the many for one week, but in the middle of the week he will put a stop to sacrifice and grain offering" – that's the first event at the midpoint; and the second is this: "and **on the wing of abominations will come one who makes desolate…**"

"On the wing of abominations" means a desecration or desolation of the Temple. The wing refers to the pinnacle of the Temple, the highest point. To desecrate means to treat a sacred place or thing with violent disrespect; to violate. To make desolate is to destroy, to ruin. The picture given is that the Temple is desecrated from the top down, so much so that the entire Temple can no longer be regarded as a holy place. The antichrist will commit an abomination that makes the entire Temple desolate.

Finally, verse 27 records that this desolation of the Temple will last until a complete destruction that is decreed is poured out on the one who makes desolate. Chapter 3 of this book will establish that this desolation of the Temple will last for the remaining 3½ years of the 70th week.

E. Summary of Daniel 9:24-27

Daniel was reading the writings of the prophet Jeremiah and realized that the 70-year captivity in Babylon was near its end. He was distressed because he knew that the discipline of the Lord has not accomplished its intended effect, which was to bring the Jews back into a proper relationship with the Lord. But he also knew that the Lord keeps His word. So Daniel engaged in an extended time of humble prayer, parts of which are recorded in chapter 9 of the book that bears his name. In response to his petitions, the angel Gabriel was sent to him with the word from the Lord that, since the 70 years of captivity had not caused the Jews to repent and return to the Lord, the Lord would keep His word of increasing the chastisement sevenfold, in accordance with Leviticus 26:18. Thus, the 70 years would be sevened, that is, multiplied by seven.

This prophecy of the 70 "sevens" of Israel's chastisement covers the total history of Israel from the time of Nehemiah in 445 B.C. until the second coming of Jesus Christ, whenever that may be. The first 69 weeks began in 445 B.C. and ended with the coming of the anointed one, the Messiah. That time period is covered in Daniel 9:25. *After* the termination of the 69th week, the Messiah was cut off – crucified – and then, approximately 40 years after that, the Temple was destroyed. The gap, the interval between the 69th and 70th weeks, began during the lifetime of Jesus Christ, before He was "cut off," and here we are, two millennia later, still in that gap. The indefinite gap is covered in Daniel 9:26. While Israel has signed treaties with many countries in the last decades, none has qualified as "the covenant" with "the prince who is to come." Therefore, the 70th week of Daniel, described in Daniel 9:27, has not yet begun.

The "prince who is to come" of verses 26 and 27 of Daniel 9 is the antichrist. He will make or confirm a covenant with Israel, which will trigger the onset of the 70th week. There will be a third Temple in Jerusalem, and the ancient Mosaic sacrificial system will be or will have been re-instituted. Three and a half years into this covenant, the antichrist will stop the sacrifices, and desecrate the Temple. Thus, the beginning of the *last* 3½ years of the 70th week of Daniel will be marked by these two things: (1) the stopping of the sacrifices in the future Temple; and (2) the desecration of that future Temple. The remainder of Daniel 9:27 says that the antichrist will continue to "make desolate" until a complete destruction that is decreed is poured out on him; that "complete destruction" will occur at the end of the 70th week.

From this review of Daniel chapter 9, there are two points to be made:

1. God cannot be finished with Israel because the 70 weeks that God decreed in Daniel 9 have not been completed. The first 69 weeks have been fulfilled, exactly as prophesied, but the fact that the 70th week has not yet happened indicates that Israel has to be around *not only* to sign the covenant *but also* for the final chastisement of God, at the end of which there will be an end of sin, and righteousness will be brought in. That's the first point: the 70 weeks are God's chastisement of Israel; the 70th week is still in the future and God is not finished with Israel.

2. It was necessary to begin this study of the Great Tribulation with the background of Daniel chapter 9 because the Great Tribulation occurs within the 70th week and because it is this 70th week of Daniel that Revelation is about, beginning with chapter 6. In this revelation to the apostle John, the Lord told him, and all of the servants of Jesus Christ from the first century forward, what this final seven-year period of this age will be like.

F. Jesus' teaching about the Great Tribulation within the 70th week

Jesus' teaching regarding the 70th week is commonly called the Olivet Discourse, because it was a teaching (discourse) on the Mount of Olives (Olivet). It is recorded in Matthew 24 and 25; parallel passages appear in Mark 13 and Luke 21. His teaching was prompted by questions His disciples had asked. These questions are recorded in Matthew 24:3: "[W]hat will be the sign of Your coming, and of the end of the age?"

Matthew 24:4-5 records: "And Jesus answered and said to them, 'See to it that no one misleads you.'" The King James Version says: "See that no one deceives you." Then the Lord proceeded to list events that would happen in the 70th week: false Christs would arise and deceive many; there would be wars and rumors of wars; and there would be famines and earthquakes in various places. But, Jesus warned, these things would be "merely the beginning of birth pangs." Beginning in Matthew 24:9, Jesus said: "Then" – meaning *after* the events which He characterized as merely the beginning of birth pangs – "they will deliver you to tribulation, and will kill you, and you will be hated by all nations on account of My name." After He described the characteristics of the Great Tribulation in the succeeding verses, He said: "Therefore" – in other words, now that I have told you how terrible the Great Tribulation will be, now I'm going to tell you when it will start and what you should do:

MATTHEW 24

> *15"Therefore, when you see the abomination of desolation which was spoken of through Daniel the prophet, standing in the holy place (let the reader understand), 16then let those who are in Judea* [Why Judea? Because Judea is where Jerusalem is, and Jerusalem is where the re-built Temple will be located, and the Temple is where the abomination of desolation will take place, so those who are in Jerusalem and the surrounding territory should] *flee to the mountains; 17let him who is on the housetop not go down to get the*

things out that are in his house; ¹⁸*and let him who is in the field not turn back to get his cloak.* ¹⁹*"But woe to those who are with child and to those who nurse babes in those days!* ²⁰*"But pray that your flight may not be in the winter, or on a Sabbath;* ²¹*for* **then** [meaning when you see the abomination of desolation standing in the holy place, that is, the Temple] *there will be a* **Great Tribulation, such as has not occurred since the beginning of the world until now, nor ever shall."**

The Lord's explicit reference in verse 15 to the prophet Daniel refers to those last four verses of Daniel chapter 9, in particular, verse 27. Jesus has tied the beginning of the Great Tribulation to the abomination of desolation standing in the holy place, that is, the Temple. That same verse, Daniel 9:27, establishes the timing of the abomination of desolation. Verse 27 says:

And he [the antichrist] *will make a firm covenant with the many* [Israel] *for* **one week** [that means for 7 years], *but* **in the middle of the week** [that means, 3 ½ years into the 7 year period], *he will put a stop to sacrifice and grain offering; and on the wing of abominations will come one* [the antichrist] *who makes desolate* [this is the reference to the "abomination of desolation"], *even until a complete destruction, one that is decreed, is poured out on the one who makes desolate."*

Tying this passage from Daniel 9 to the teaching of Jesus in Matthew 24 leads to the conclusion that the Great Tribulation will begin at the midpoint of Daniel's 70th week. Since the 70th week is a period of seven years, that means that the Great Tribulation will begin 3½ years into the seven-year period. And that brings us full circle back to the beginning of this chapter.

G. Biblical names for the 70th week

The title of this chapter asks: "What IS this tribulation period?" In order to avoid mis-communication and confusion, it is important for everyone to be on the same Biblical page, so to speak, when it comes to the terminology of the end times. Many people refer to the whole of Daniel's 70th week as the "tribulation period." The problem with that terminology is that is does not line up with the teaching of Jesus Christ Himself. Jesus never taught that the entire seven years of the 70th week will be a time of tribulation. In Matthew 24, Jesus described the first 3½ years as a time of "the beginning of birth pangs" or "the beginning of sorrows." He never called it a time of tribulation. He did, however, describe the *second* 3½-year period as the *Great Tribulation*. The combination of Daniel 9:27 with Matthew 24:15-22, leads to the conclusion that the Great Tribulation begins at the midpoint of the 70th week.

What this means is that the entire seven years is not a time of tribulation, and it is inaccurate Biblically to call the 70th week "the tribulation period." The only accurate terms for the entire seven-year period are either "Daniel's 70th week," or simply "the 70th week."

It is the 70th week that Revelation describes in some detail, beginning at chapter 6.

Summary: The antichrist will make or confirm a covenant with Israel, the majority of whom will still be living in unbelief, for a period of seven years. This will initiate Daniel's 70th week. The events that will take place during the first half, or 3½ years, Jesus called "the beginning of birth pangs." Halfway through this period of 7 years, that is, 3½ years into it, the antichrist will break the covenant, enter the rebuilt Temple in Jerusalem, put a stop to the sacrifice and grain offerings, and set up or commit the abomination of desolation. This will trigger the Great Tribulation, so terrible in its scope that Jesus described it in Matthew

24:21-22, as one "such as has not occurred since the beginning of the world until now, nor ever shall." The persecution of Jews and Christians in the Great Tribulation will be so viciously successful that, "unless those days had been cut short, no life would have been saved; but for the sake of the elect those days shall be cut short." (Matthew 24:22)

• 2 •

Is the Great Tribulation relevant to Christians?

A. Setting the stage in Revelation: the scroll with seven seals

As Revelation 4 opens, John is ushered into the throne room of heaven itself. In this chapter and in Revelation 5, which is a continuation of chapter 4, John attempts to describe in human language the indescribable beauty of heaven. Because the focus of this book is limited to the Great Tribulation on earth, the possible symbolism employed in chapters 4 and 5 will not be addressed.

John sees God the Father sitting on the throne, surrounded by 24 thrones with 24 elders. Immediately around the throne, apparently the closest to it, are the four living creatures. There is a rainbow around the throne, which John describes as emerald in appearance. The four living creatures are worshiping God by praising His holiness. The 24 elders join in, falling down before the Lord and casting their crowns before the throne.

While chapter 4 focuses on a description of the throne room itself and the worship of God by the other occupants of the room, in chapter 5 there is additional activity. John notices that God the Father holds a scroll, which is written on both sides, and rolled up and sealed with seven seals. Then John sees – and hears, obviously – a strong angel proclaiming with a loud voice: "Who is worthy to open the scroll and to break its seals?" But no one in heaven or on earth or under the earth is worthy to open the scroll and to look into it. John begins to weep greatly; why? Why is it so important that the seals on the scroll be broken and the scroll be opened? Because of what the scroll represents.

In the Roman Empire, which was ruling at the time that John was writing, last wills and testaments were sealed with seven seals, and only the person or persons authorized to do so could break the seals and learn what their inheritance consisted of. If, for example, the person who wrote the will, the testator, had left his land to his son, then this will would be the authoritative document which would transfer title to the land from the deceased father to the living son. The scroll sealed with the seven seals in Revelation 5 was a similar document, and for that reason, some commentators call it a last will and testament.

Others, however, call it a contract or a deed of purchase. Their reasoning is that a purchase was made at the cross, and now the deed of that purchase must be claimed by its rightful owner. Thus, the scroll of Revelation chapter 5 contains the title deed to the planet earth; in other words, the land or the property that was purchased is the planet earth as well as its inhabitants.

Not only do most, if not all, commentators agree that the scroll of Revelation 5 either is or contains the title deed to the planet earth, they also agree that the contents of the scroll do not describe *what* is covered, like a metes and bounds description of land; rather, the contents of the scroll describe *how* dominion over the earth will be taken from the usurper and trespasser, Satan, and restored to its rightful owner, God the Son, who has qualified and become worthy to take and open the scroll by becoming the perfect Lamb who was slain for the sins of the world. Thus, *the contents of the scroll describe the judgments that God will execute upon the earth and its unrepentant inhabitants.* When the seals are all broken so that the scroll can be opened and looked into, the following chapters of Revelation reveal that the contents of this scroll are God's final judgments. The time period in which these judgments will be administered is known throughout the Old Testament and the

New Testament as the "Day of the Lord." Therefore, a shorthand way of describing the contents of the scroll is the Day of the Lord.

Chapter 6 continues to describe the activity in the throne room of heaven. Having taken the scroll sealed with the seven seals, the Lamb begins to break them, so that He can open the scroll and look into it. Six of the seven seals are broken in this chapter 6.

With the breaking of the first seal, the 70th week of Daniel begins. This is the "week," or period of seven years, that is described in Daniel 9:27. That verse explains that what triggers the onset of the 70th week is the making of or the strengthening of a covenant between the antichrist ("the prince who is to come" of verse 26; and "he" of verse 27) and Israel ("the many" of verse 27). Thus, the making of the covenant of Daniel 9:27 is related to the first seal of Revelation chapter 6.

In other words, the 70th week is triggered by an event in heaven with a corresponding event on earth. When, in heaven, the Lord breaks the first seal on the scroll of Revelation, the corresponding event on the earth is the making of, or the strengthening of, the covenant described in Daniel 9:27, between the antichrist and Israel.

B. The parallels between Revelation 6 and Matthew 24

These two corresponding events, one in heaven (the breaking of the first seal) and the other on earth (the making of the covenant of Daniel 9:27), are also tied to the Olivet Discourse of Matthew 24 and 25, in which Jesus Christ described Daniel's 70th week. The Lord's revelation to John, beginning with chapter 6 of Revelation, parallels His description of approximately 60 years earlier in the Olivet Discourse that is recorded in the synoptic Gospels. In other words, there are parallels between the seals of Revelation 6 and the Lord's teaching in the Olivet Discourse of Matthew 24 and 25, Mark 13, and Luke 21.

Matthew 24:4-8 describes the first four seals of Revelation 6.

1. The First Seal: The Antichrist

After His warning not to be deceived or misled, the Lord began His teaching by saying, in Matthew 24:5: "For many will come in My name, saying, 'I am the Christ,' and will mislead many." The parallel passage given to John some 60 years later appears in Revelation 6:1 and 2, which report that the first seal is the white horse with a rider who has a bow – but notice he has no arrows to go with the bow – and he is given a crown, and he goes out conquering and to conquer.

What does this white horse and rider represent? In the Bible, particularly in Revelation, white is a symbol for purity and righteousness, but in this case, the righteousness is only on the surface. This rider on the white horse is not the same rider on the white horse of Revelation 19. In verse 11 it says that He who sat upon the white horse is called Faithful and True, and His name is called The Word of God. Clearly, this is Jesus Christ. But a quick comparison with chapter 6 demonstrates that these are different identities. The rider of the white horse in chapter 6 is wearing a crown, singular, and the Greek word used there for crown is *stefanos*; it represents, for example, the crown that a champion in athletic games might win. In contrast, in Revelation 19:11-13, the rider of this white horse has on His head many diadems. As the use of the English word, diadems, indicates, the Greek word here is not *stefanos*, but *diadema*, which is the crown of royalty. Thus, not only are there two different kinds of crowns, but also the rider in chapter 6 has only one of the first kind, whereas the rider in chapter 19 has multiple crowns of the second kind.

Another difference is that the rider in chapter 6 carries a bow, whereas Jesus Christ in chapter 19 has a sharp sword issuing from His mouth. Moreover, the rider in chapter 6 appears alone, but Jesus Christ rides out of heaven in chapter 19 followed by the armies which are in heaven, and they are also riding white horses. Therefore, the rider of the white horse in Revelation 6:2 is not Jesus Christ. Who, then, is he? Most commentators agree that this rider represents the culmination of many false messiahs over the course of history in this final antichrist, who rides a white horse because he *deceives the nations* into believing that he is the Messiah, the political savior of mankind. After all, isn't that what we expect at the end of a movie that shows a great conflict between good and evil – that the hero will ride in on a white horse to save the day? But it is important to know that the primary tool of the antichrist will be deception. His white horse, a symbol of majestic righteousness, will be nothing more than show, which is meant to, and which will, deceive the world. The antichrist is not only against Christ; he will want to take the place of Christ. He will be a counterfeit parallel to Jesus Christ, a counterfeit who deceives the world. Jesus alluded to this counterfeit in John 5:43: "I have come in My Father's name, and you do not receive Me; if another shall come in his own name, you will receive him."

Revelation 6:2 records that he goes out conquering, present tense, and to conquer, future tense, but how does he do this with the bow but no arrows? The answer is that he conquers without the use of force; perhaps the presence of the bow is the threat of force, although those who know the text of Revelation will know that it would be an empty threat, because he has no arrows.

Because the 70th week, the final seven years of this present age, will begin with the signing of a covenant brokered by the antichrist between Israel and other nations, it may be that the accomplishment of this treaty is sufficient to bring peace, however temporary and however false, to the tumultuous Middle East – and for that the antichrist will be hailed by the world as a savior. Remember that he is riding on a white horse; the Jews of Israel and those in the rest of the world who have not studied Revelation will be deceived into believing that he is a righteous man and more. Completely deceived and taken in, the world will believe he is the savior of mankind. They will not know that he is the antichrist. They will not know that he operates on behalf of Satan. They will not know that his ultimate goal is the annihilation of all Jews and all Christians, so that Jesus Christ will have no kingdom to rule over.

Summary: The breaking of the first seal of Revelation 6 in heaven corresponds to the appearance of the antichrist on the earth.

2. The second seal: war

At the breaking of the second seal, John sees a red horse, and its rider is allowed to take peace from the earth so that men would slay one another, and this rider is given a great sword. Clearly, this is a description of war. Note the passive voice. The rider *was allowed* to take peace from the earth. Throughout the book of Revelation, the sovereignty of the Lord is emphasized everywhere. The same Greek word that is translated as "red" is also used to describe the dragon (who represents Satan) in chapter 12:3. It is flame-colored, a fiery red.

The passage from the Olivet Discourse in Matthew 24, which corresponds to the second seal, appears in verses 6 and 7: "And you will be hearing of wars and rumors of wars; see that you are not frightened, for those things must take place, but that is not yet the end. For nation will rise against nation, and kingdom against kingdom…"

Summary: The breaking of the second seal of Revelation 6 in heaven corresponds to war on earth.

3. The third seal: famine

The Lord continued in Matthew 24:7: "…and in various places there will be famines…" Those who have lived through World War II know that war leads to shortages of food and supplies, and these wars will be no different. This characteristic of the 70th week corresponds with the third seal of Revelation 6, which is a black horse and rider who has a pair of scales in his hand. John hears something like a voice which says: "a quart of wheat for a denarius, and three quarts of barley for a denarius; and do not damage [or waste] the oil and the wine." A denarius was a day's pay for the average worker. One quart of wheat a day was barely enough for one person to stay alive. Barley was a little cheaper, but it was also less nourishing. The pair of scales in the hand of the rider indicates rationing of food during this severe famine. The high cost of food indicates meager crops and scarcity of food. Thus, this seal represents the famine and economic deprivation that would follow on the heels of war.

Summary: The breaking of the third seal of Revelation 6 in heaven corresponds to famine on earth.

4. THE FOURTH SEAL: DEATH AND HADES

When the Lamb breaks the fourth seal, John sees an ashen horse; in some translations it is called a pale horse. The rider of this pale horse is named death, and hades is following with him. It seems that in this vision, both death and hades are personified, and they are either riding together on this horse, or hades is following behind the horse on foot. Authority is given to them over a fourth of the earth. Again, note the passive voice: authority *was given* to them; just as Satan's harassment of Job was circumscribed by God, the Lord remains sovereign at all times.

Careful observation becomes critically important in another part of this verse 8 as well. The text does not say that a fourth of the *population* of the earth will be killed. It says that death and hades have authority over a fourth of *the earth*. This sounds as if they have authority over one fourth of the geographical land masses of the earth. That this may be what is meant seems to be confirmed by the fact that, at the sixth trumpet, one third of *mankind* is killed (Revelation 9:15). The reference in Revelation 6:8, to *the earth itself* rather than to *mankind* must be significant. Nevertheless, it is important to remember that, since death has held sway over *all the earth* since the fall of Adam, verse 8 can hardly mean the death of people in only one quarter of the world's countries. Death is, after all, universal.

An examination of the rest of this verse 8 may shed some light. "Authority was given to them over a fourth of the earth, to kill with sword and with famine and with pestilence and by the wild beasts of the earth." The Greek word that is translated into English as "pestilence" in the NASB is *thanatos*, which means death. In fact, this Greek word *thanatos* appears twice in this verse 8.

Here is the whole verse in the NASB:

"And I looked, and behold, an ashen horse; and he who sat on it had the name **Death/thanatos***; and Hades was following with him. And authority was given to them over a fourth of the earth, to kill with sword and with famine and with* **pestilence/thanatos** *and by the wild beasts of the earth."*

Therefore, what this verse actually says is: **Death/thanatos** was riding the fourth horse and authority was given to kill with sword and with famine and with **death/thanatos**, *not* pestilence.

Still in Revelation 6:8, the word that is translated into English in the NASB as "wild beasts" is *therion*, and it means a dangerous animal. This same Greek word is used 38 other times in the book of Revelation, and in every other instance it refers either to the first beast of Revelation 13, who is the antichrist, or to the second beast of Revelation 13, who is later called the false prophet. Moreover, here in Revelation 6:8, the definite article "the" is used before the word for beasts. Thus, "*the beasts of the earth*," seems to be a reference to the first and the second beasts of Revelation, meaning the antichrist and his false prophet.

One final point about this verse 8 is to consider what is being referred to when the verse says, "authority was given to *them*." At first glance, it appears to be saying that authority was given to death and hades. While that may indeed be the case, the fact remains that death is universal, not limited to either one fourth of the world's population or to one fourth of the world's land masses. Consider the possibility that the word, "them," refers to all four horses. Verse 8 says that authority was given to *them* over a fourth of the earth,

- to kill with sword – that's the second horse, the red horse, which represents war;

- to kill with famine – that's the third horse, the black horse, which represents famine;
- to kill with death – remember that the Greek word there is *thanatos*, and is properly translated as "death," not as "pestilence." This would be this fourth horse, which represents death and hades;
- and to kill by the beasts of the earth – that's the *first horse*, the white one, with the rider that represents the antichrist, who is called elsewhere in Revelation the first beast, and the second beast, who is later called the false prophet.

How would death result from the first seal, which represents the antichrist? The answer is, through his use of the second, third, and fourth seals: death by war (the second seal); death by famine (the third seal); and death by "death and hades" (the fourth seal). This last one requires further explanation.

Robert Van Kampen, writing on the subject of this fourth seal, takes the position in his book, *The Sign* (Second Edition, 1993, at pages 249-250), that death and hades are depicted together in this fourth seal because they will represent the *choice* that every Christian will have to make during the Great Tribulation, when they are being persecuted by the antichrist. The choice will be to submit to the mark of the beast and worship his image *or* be killed. Those who refuse to take the mark and to worship the image of the beast will have chosen *death*, but that death will be a glorious entrance into the presence of Jesus Christ in heaven. Conversely, those who submit to the mark of the beast and worship his image will not die immediately but will have chosen *hades*, and ultimately hell, the lake of fire.

Since unbelievers will have no problem taking the mark of the beast and worshiping his image, it is *only believers* who will be forced to decide whether or not to submit to the mark of the beast and to worship his image. If they do, they will have chosen to spend an eternity in hell; their only other choice will be to be killed. Since this verse 8 gives death and hades authority over one fourth of the earth, Van Kampen thinks this is a reference to Christians worldwide.

According to the Pew Research Center, as of 2013, there are approximately 2.18 billion Christians in the world today, which is approximately 32% of the world's population, significantly higher that the 25% (which would be 1.75 billion) of the fourth seal of Revelation 6. Of the 2.18 billion who claim to be Christians, however, not all are; Jesus taught that there are tares among the wheat (Matthew 13:24-43), and those will not choose death but will choose hades. One has to wonder whether 1.75 billion of the 2.18 billion are true Christians. Until the time that they are rounded up and forced to choose between taking the mark of the beast or being killed, however, Christians will not be able to buy or sell, so it is foreseeable that they would suffer from famine in the meantime.

The bottom line is that the interpretation of Revelation 6:8 depends upon whether one fourth of the earth means geographical territory or population. In either event, the picture is truly disturbing. Nevertheless, Jesus said, in Matthew 24:8: "All these things are merely the beginning of birth pangs."

All of the first four seals—false Christs, wars and rumors of wars, famine, and death as a result of the prior three, as well as death by plagues, by genocide, by earthquakes or other natural disasters—are nothing new in the history of mankind. For that reason, scholars have been quick to point out the increasing frequency of natural disasters and of wars, with their attendant manifestations of suffering. But it is important to remember that these seals refer to events that will occur *within* the 70th week of Daniel. That seven-year period will be triggered in the visible, earthly realm by the making or strengthening of an agreement between Israel and the antichrist *and*, in the invisible, heavenly realm by the Lord Jesus' breaking of the first seal on the scroll, as described in Revelation 6. Until that time, the increasing frequency of natural disasters and of wars, in and of themselves, are not a sign that we are in the very end of days.

Summary: The breaking of the fourth seal of Revelation 6 in heaven corresponds to death on earth, due to famine (the third seal); due to

war (the second seal); and due to the persecution of the antichrist and his false prophet (the first seal).

5. The Fifth Seal: Martyrs Under the Altar

The fourth seal not only relates back to the prior three seals, but it is also connected to the fifth seal, which represents the martyrs under the altar.

When the Lamb breaks the fifth seal, John sees "underneath the altar" martyred souls. They were persecuted, according to Revelation 6:6, "because of the word of God, and because of the testimony which they had maintained." These martyrs under the altar cry out with a loud voice asking the Lord how long He will refrain from avenging their blood on "those who dwell on the earth." This phrase, or variations of it, is a key phrase used throughout the book of Revelation to describe unbelievers. Sometimes they are called the inhabitants of the earth, or the inhabitants who dwell upon the earth, or simply those who dwell upon the earth. Thus, these martyrs under the altar were killed by unbelievers for the very reason that they were believers, and they know that God has not yet judged the unbelievers. Apparently, a number of additional believers are to be martyred, however, so these are given a white robe and told to rest. The white robe represents the righteousness of Christ which is imputed to believers.

Notice the location of the martyrs: under the altar. The altar was a place of sacrifice. Romans 12:1 exhorts believers to present their bodies a living and holy sacrifice, acceptable to God, which is their spiritual service of worship. These special martyrs have been more than living sacrifices; their very lives were sacrificed for the name of Jesus.

The parallel in Matthew 24 for the fifth seal of Revelation 6 is the Great Tribulation. It is possible that both the fourth and fifth seals are representative of the Great Tribulation. There is no doubt that death (the fourth seal) will be a prominent characteristic of the Great Tribulation. Jesus certainly connected the two; He said, in Matthew 24:9: "Then they will deliver you to tribulation, and *will kill you*, and you will be hated by all nations *on account of My name.*" That is exactly what the fifth seal describes in Revelation 6:9: believers who are killed "because of the word of God, and because of the testimony that they had maintained."

Lest there be any doubt remaining regarding the severity of this persecution, the Lord described it in Matthew 24:21-22 as "a great tribulation, such as has not occurred since the beginning of the world until now, nor ever shall. And unless those days had been cut short, *no life would have been saved*; but for the sake of the elect those days shall be cut short."

Even those among us who have not endured the arduous process of labor and delivery know that labor pains begin slowly, but then they increase in frequency and intensity as labor progresses. Similarly, in the second half of the 70th week, the unfolding events will speed up and become more intense. At the midpoint of the 70th week, this is no longer "merely the beginning of birth pangs." This is hard labor. This is all-out tribulation. Great tribulation.

It is the time that the antichrist will go after the Jews in a worldwide holocaust that will make that of World War II pale by comparison. But Jews will not be the only target of the antichrist's persecution. In Matthew 24, Jesus was speaking to *believers*. While it is true that the first believers, the first Christians, were Jews, the commands that Jesus gave to His disciples, such as the memorial of the Last Supper, and the great commission, were intended not for Jews, but for Christians. Confirmation of the fact that Christians will also be targeted in the Great Tribulation comes from the fact that Jesus said, in Matthew 24:22, that, "unless those days had been cut short, no life would have been saved; but *for the sake of the elect* those days shall be cut short." The "elect" is a reference to believers. Moreover, in Revelation 12, when Satan is permanently evicted from the premises of heaven, he has great wrath and persecutes "the woman," a reference to faithful Jews; but when he is thwarted in his attempts to annihilate those Jews, he goes after Christians, who are described in Revelation 12:17 as "the rest of her offspring, who keep the commandments of God and hold to the testimony of Jesus."

II Thessalonians 2, describing the antichrist as the "man of lawlessness" and the "son of destruction," says that he will oppose and exalt himself above every so-called god or object of worship, so that he takes his seat in the Temple of God, displaying himself as being God. Many scholars believe that this blasphemous act is THE abomination of desolation, and, if that is correct, then this is what will happen in the middle of Daniel's 70th week. Having set himself up as God, the antichrist will demand the world's worship, and that is when all the Christians of the world will have to choose whether to bow the knee to the antichrist and to take his mark *or* to be executed for refusing to do so.

Since the fourth seal represents death and hades, the fifth seal is a logical consequence. The fifth seal represents the martyrs under the altar, those believers who were "slain because of the word of God, and because of the testimony which they had maintained" (Revelation 6:9). The fifth seal appears to be a picture of all the Christians who are slaughtered during the time of the Great Tribulation for refusing to bow to the antichrist and to take his mark.

Summary: The breaking of the fifth seal of Revelation 6 in heaven corresponds to the Great Tribulation on earth, which begins at the midpoint of the 70th week.

Summary of the first five seals of Revelation 6: The antichrist will make or confirm a covenant with Israel, the majority of whom will still be living in unbelief, for a period of seven years. This will initiate Daniel's 70th week. In heaven, the Lord Jesus will begin breaking the seals on the scroll which He took from the hand of God the Father in Revelation 5. The events that will take place during the first half, or 3½ years, Jesus called in Matthew 24 "the beginning of birth pangs." Those events will include wars and rumors of wars, famine, and death. Halfway through this period of 7 years, that is, 3½ years into it, the antichrist will break the covenant, will enter the rebuilt Temple in Jerusalem, put a stop to the sacrifice and grain offerings, and set up or commit the abomination of desolation. He will desecrate the Temple by setting himself up as God and demanding that the world worship him as God. This will trigger the Great Tribulation, the time when all peoples and tribes and nations and tongues will be given over to the power of the antichrist, and he will viciously persecute the Jews and also the followers of Jesus.

This time of the Great Tribulation, the latter half of Daniel's 70th week, will last for close to 3½ years, and is also known in other books of the Bible as "a time, times, and half a time," and as 42 months, and as 1260 days. The Great Tribulation will be so horrific that the antichrist, who will have been invested with the power and authority of Satan himself, will come very close to achieving his goal of murdering every living Jew and Christian. Before he does, however, the Lord will cut those days of the Great Tribulation short. The days of the 70th week will continue on, but the days of the Great Tribulation will be cut short.

Because of the unparalleled reign of terror of the antichrist, Jesus reiterated His warnings to His disciples, and, through them, to us. In Matthew 24:23-26, the Lord cautioned: "Then if anyone says to you, 'Behold, here is the Christ,' or 'There He is,' do not believe him. For false Christs and false prophets will arise and will show great signs and wonders, so as to mislead, if possible, even the elect. Behold, I have told you in advance. If therefore they say to you, 'Behold, He is in the wilderness,' do not go forth, or, 'Behold, He is in the inner rooms,' do not believe them." The level of deception during this dangerous time in history will run so deep that many learned and knowledgeable people, including some leaders in the Church, will be deceived. It will be only by the grace of God that the elect will stand firm. The phrase, "if it were possible," implies that it is not possible for the elect to be deceived because the elect are kept by the power of God.

Having just warned His followers, in verse 26, not to believe those who say that He has arrived but is out in the wilderness or that He is in the inner rooms, Jesus then describes His return in Matthew 24:27-31. Verse 27 says: "For just as the lightning comes from the east, and flashes even to the west, so shall the coming of the Son of Man be." This means that, when He comes, He will not come secretly and stay hidden from public view. Instead, He will appear like a flash of lightning: suddenly, and visible to everyone. Revelation 1:7 says the same thing: "Behold, He is coming with the clouds, and *every eye will see Him*."

Matthew 24:28 really reinforces the point that Jesus is making here, but to many of us, it comes as a jolt, this verse that just seems to be stuck in the middle of this passage, with no relevance whatever to the passage. Verse 28 says: "Wherever the corpse is, there the vultures will gather." This was apparently a saying or a proverb. There are many interpretations about its meaning in this context, but the simplest is that, just as people can see from far away the vultures that are circling up in the air, Christ's return will be visible to all. One other interpretation is that the vultures represent the widespread death that will accompany the return of Christ as King and Judge of the unrighteous. But even in that case, everyone will still see Him when He comes.

Now, having specified *how* He will return, that is, suddenly and visible to everyone, Jesus sets out in Matthew 24:29 *when* He will return, in general terms, and this leads to the sixth seal of Revelation.

6. The Sixth Seal: Cataclysmic Upheavals in the Heavens and on Earth

When the Lamb breaks the sixth seal, there are huge cosmic disturbances. The sun becomes black as sackcloth, and the moon becomes like blood; the stars of the sky fall to the earth, and the sky is split apart like a scroll when it is rolled up. Back on the earth, there is a tremendous earthquake, so intense that all mountains and islands are moved out of their places. At this point, men try to hide in the caves and among the rocks of the mountains, because, according to Revelation 6:16-17, they want to hide from "Him who sits on the throne and from the wrath of the Lamb; for the great day of their wrath has come, and who is able to stand?"

This sixth seal parallels the next portion of Jesus' teaching in the Olivet Discourse. In Matthew 24:29-31, the Lord stated: "Immediately *after* the tribulation of those days the sun will be darkened, and the moon will not give its light, and the stars will fall from the sky, and the powers of the heavens will be shaken, and then the sign of the Son of Man will appear in the sky, and then all the tribes of the earth will mourn, and they will see the Son of Man coming on the clouds of the sky with power and great glory. And He will send forth His angels with a great trumpet and they will gather together His elect from the four winds, from one end of the sky to the other."

Summary of the sixth seal of Revelation 6: The passage in Matthew 24:27-31 teaches that the Lord will come again *after* the Great Tribulation; it is after the Great Tribulation because it is He who will cut short the days of the Great Tribulation by His appearance (Matthew 24:22ff). His coming will be preceded by the cataclysmic upheavals in the heavens and on the earth that will extinguish all natural light in the heavens and plunge the earth into total darkness. These upheavals will be the sign of the end of the age. The black darkness will be broken by the supernatural light of the Lord as He comes to gather together His own in the rapture.

Matthew 24:30-31 describes the rapture of believers, both those who have died prior to the Lord's return and those who have somehow survived the Great Tribulation. The rapture is described in the next chapter of Revelation, chapter 7, verses 9 through 17. The subject of the rapture will be covered in chapter 4 of this book.

C. The relationship between the 70th week and God's wrath in the Day of the Lord

Many evangelical Christians today believe that the seals on the outside of the scroll of Revelation 5 are part of God's final outpouring of wrath in that period of time known throughout the Bible as the Day of the

Lord. If they were, then the rapture of believers prior to the onset of the 70th week, when the first seal is broken, would be Biblically supportable. The entire purpose of this book, however, is to demonstrate that, because the seals are *not* part of God's wrath in the Day of the Lord, believers *will* be present on the earth during the Great Tribulation, and will not be raptured off the earth until after the sixth seal. Below are some of the reasons why the seals cannot be properly characterized as the Day of the Lord in the sense of God's final wrath.

1. In His Day of the Lord wrath, the Lord will avenge the blood of every martyr. Since, as of the time of the fifth seal, He has not yet done so, the Day of the Lord cannot have begun before the fifth seal.

The fifth seal represents the martyrs under the altar, believers who are being killed precisely because they are followers of Jesus Christ. If this fifth seal were the time of God's final wrath, then God would be killing off His own children, through the agency of the antichrist; but this cannot be the case, because the martyrs are asking God to *avenge their deaths* at the hands of the unbelievers who are known as those who dwell upon the earth. Because the judgment of the Lord is always just and true, they could hardly be asking Him to avenge their deaths if He were responsible for their deaths.

When the Day of the Lord *does* commence, *then* the Lord will avenge the blood of every saint and martyr. Because the martyrs are asking the Lord how long He will continue *to refrain from* judging and avenging their blood on those who dwell upon the earth, that means that, at the time of this fifth seal, He has not yet done it. Therefore, the Day of the Lord cannot have yet begun.

Two passages from Paul's epistles reinforce the conclusion that the fifth seal cannot be God's wrath. I Thessalonians 5:9 assures believers that "God has not destined us for wrath, but for obtaining salvation through our Lord Jesus Christ." Romans 5:9 reiterates this point: "having now been justified by His blood, we shall be saved from the wrath of God through Him." The principle is clear: believers will be *spared* the wrath of God that is poured out in the Day of the Lord. But these martyrs under the altar were *not spared* the wrath of someone because Revelation 6:9 states explicitly that they were "slain because of the word of God and because of the testimony which they had maintained" – meaning they were slain precisely because they were Christians; therefore, this cannot be *God's wrath*, the final wrath from which believers will be spared.

2. If the Great Tribulation were God's wrath, Jesus would not have told anyone to flee when it begins.

Jesus explained in Matthew 24:15 that the Great Tribulation would be triggered by the abomination of desolation spoken of by Daniel the prophet. Tying in Daniel 9:27 leads to the conclusion that this Great Tribulation will begin at the midpoint of the 70th week. Then Jesus warns those in and around Jerusalem *to flee*. If the Great Tribulation were God's wrath, the only appropriate response to His wrath would be to fall on one's face in repentance, not to flee. Besides, it would be impossible, indeed, it *will* be impossible to flee from or hide from God's wrath when it comes.

3. If the Great Tribulation were God's wrath, then the Lord would not have to cut it short.

In Matthew 24:21-22, Jesus taught: "For then there will be a great tribulation, such as has not occurred since the beginning of the world until now, nor ever shall. And **unless those days had been cut short,** no life would have been saved; but **for the sake of the elect those days shall be cut short.**"

It is for the sake of the elect (believers) that the Lord cuts short the days of the Great Tribulation. If the Great Tribulation were a manifestation of His own wrath, He would not need to intervene to cut it short. God needs no correction or intervention into His dealings with mankind.

Moreover, the fact that the Lord has to cut short the days of the Great Tribulation for the sake of the elect plainly implies that the elect (believers) are still on the earth. If the Great Tribulation were the wrath of God, then what are His elect still doing on the earth? They are promised exemption from His wrath. Their presence on the earth during the Great Tribulation, therefore, means that the Great Tribulation cannot be God's wrath.

This promise (that the elect – believers – will not be on the earth during the Day of the Lord wrath) was taught and understood in the earliest days of the Church. Indeed, it was the knowledge of this promise that caused the uproar in the Thessalonian church and prompted Paul's second epistle to them. The Thessalonians had received a forged or fake letter that purported to be from Paul; the gist of the fake letter was that the Day of the Lord had already begun. As a result, the Thessalonian believers, knowing they should have been raptured off the earth before the onset of the Day of the Lord, were naturally "shaken from their composure" because they believed that they had been truly left behind. The epistle we know as II Thessalonians was written primarily to reassure the distressed believers that the Day of the Lord had not yet come.

4. The first seal represents the emergence of a final world ruler, and his rule over the world would be inconsistent with the exaltation of the Lord *alone* in the Day of the Lord.

In *that* time, God alone will be exalted, and all proud men will be abased. *See*, for example, the following citations: Isaiah 2:12,17,19-21; 13:9-13; Jeremiah 46:10; Ezekiel 7:7-11; 30:3,8; 38:23; Joel 2:10-11; Zephaniah 3:8; Zechariah 14:1-9; and Revelation 6:17. In fact, according to Revelation 6:17 and Joel 2:11, no one will be *able* to stand against Him. For that reason, it is completely contradictory that, during this same time, God would allow the ultimate Satan-inspired and possibly Satan-possessed blasphemer to "oppose and exalt *himself* above every so-called god or object of worship, so that he takes his seat in the Temple of God, displaying *himself* as being God." That's from II Thessalonians 2:4; Daniel 11:36 says something very similar: "he will exalt and magnify himself above every god, and will speak monstrous things against the God of gods."

The antichrist simply could not rise to power, consolidate the entire world into his *own* kingdom under his *own* authority, commit the abomination of desolation in the rebuilt Temple in Jerusalem, declare *himself* to be God, demand that the world worship *him* as God, and immediately thereafter begin slaughtering Jews and Christians wholesale – all during the time period known as the Day of the Lord, because the Lord alone will be exalted in that day. The only possible conclusion is that those events, those actions by the antichrist, will precede the Day of the Lord.

The same principle applies to the fifth seal: because the antichrist will be executing Christians and Jews on an unprecedented scale, it is clear that he will be exalting himself. Once the Day of the Lord begins, however, even the antichrist will be rendered powerless, as the Lord alone will be exalted in that time period.

5. Jesus taught in Matthew 24 that the events that are paralleled by the seals of Revelation 6 are "the beginning of birth pangs" and "the Great Tribulation," not the wrath of God.

Nowhere in that teaching of Matthew 24 did Jesus say that these events are His wrath. Moreover, while Jesus taught His followers about events that paralleled the seals of Revelation 6, conspicuous by its absence is any mention by Jesus in Matthew 24 of any events that would have paralleled the trumpets and the bowls of Revelation. Since the trumpets and bowls do represent the final wrath of God, the followers of Jesus would not need to be warned about those.

6. The wrath of God is mentioned eight times in Revelation, but never before the sixth seal is broken.

The first time in Revelation that the wrath of God is mentioned is in 6:16, at the time of the sixth seal. The word "wrath" appears an additional seven times in the book of Revelation, but never before this point. There is no reason to make it retroactive to cover the prior seals.

7. Since the 144,000 are sealed so that they will be protected from the judgments of the Day of the Lord, then the Day of the Lord cannot begin before they are sealed, which is after the sixth seal.

After the breaking of the sixth seal, but before the breaking of the seventh, Revelation 7:2-4 records an angel having the "seal" of the living God, crying out "with a loud voice to the four angels to whom it was granted to harm the earth and the sea, saying, 'Do not harm the earth or the sea or the trees, until we have sealed the bond-servants of our God on their foreheads.' And I heard the number of those who were sealed, one hundred and forty-four thousand sealed from every tribe of the sons of Israel."

Unlike those who will have taken the mark of the beast on their foreheads or hands, these 144,000 Jews will receive the seal of God on their foreheads, so that they will not be harmed by the coming judgment of God. The text plainly states that, after these people are sealed, God, through His angels, is about to harm the land and the sea and the trees—a good description of the trumpet judgments (part of the Day of the Lord) about to commence.

Since the 144,000 are sealed so that they will be protected during the Day of the Lord, then the Day of the Lord cannot begin before that time. The sealing of the 144,000 just prior to the onset of judgment is logical, unlike sealing them well after judgment has begun. Since they are sealed after the sixth seal, and just before the seventh seal is broken and the scroll is opened, the Day of the Lord cannot begin before that time;

therefore, the seals are not part of the Day of the Lord judgment from which believers are promised exemption.

D. The presence of Christians on earth during the Great Tribulation

There is nothing in the Bible which promises that Christians will be spared suffering. On the contrary, believers should expect trial, persecution, and suffering. *See*, for example, these citations: Acts 14:22; II Corinthians 6:3-10; Ephesians 6:11-13; Philippians 1:29-30 and 3:10-11; Colossians 1:24; I Thessalonians 3:3-4; II Thessalonians 1:4-5; II Timothy 1:8,12; 2:3; 2:9; and 3:12; I Peter 2:20 and 4:12-14; Revelation 2:10. Certainly Jesus was not spared the full wrath of His Father at the cross. But what Jesus did tell His followers, in John 16:33, is this: "These things I have spoken to you, so that in Me, you may have peace. In the world, you have tribulation, but take courage; I have overcome the world."

What Christians *are* promised is exemption from the final wrath of God in the Day of the Lord. According to I Thessalonians 1:10, Jesus "delivers us from the wrath to come." Later, in the same letter, Paul wrote (5:9): "For God has not destined us for wrath, but for obtaining salvation through our Lord Jesus Christ." This promise also appears in Romans 5:9: "…having now been justified by His blood, we shall be saved from the wrath of God through Him." The fact that the seals of Revelation 6 are *not* His final wrath, however, means that the events which the seals unleash will occur while Christians are still on the earth, *before* the rapture. Therefore, wisdom dictates that all believers learn as much as possible about this one-world dictator, the antichrist, before he arrives on the scene. He is the subject of the next chapter of this book.

Summary: Since the teaching of Matthew 24 tracks the breaking of the seals of Revelation 6, including the rapture right after the breaking of the sixth seal, the Great Tribulation is not only relevant, but critically important for Christians to understand. Because many Christians today have been taught that all believers will be removed from the earth and taken to heaven before the events of Revelation 6-22 occur, they will be caught unprepared to deal with the demands of the antichrist in the Great Tribulation. This will be an unparalled time of terror, when all who call themselves Christians will have to choose whether to bow the knee to the antichrist and worship him as God, or to be executed for their refusal to do so. True Christians will suffer horribly the wrath of Satan, as he acts through his human agent, the antichrist, in this Great Tribulation, but their deliverance through the rapture and the final outpouring of the wrath of God will not come until the Lord decides to cut the days of the Great Tribulation short for the sake of the elect. Jesus described what will happen to many people who consider themselves to be Christians, in Matthew 24:10-12: "At that time many will fall away and will deliver up one another and hate one another. And many false prophets will arise, and will mislead many. And because lawlessness is increased, most people's love will grow cold." It is my prayer that no reader of this book will be included in that description.

• 3 •

WHO IS THE ANTICHRIST?

A. Origin of the term "antichrist"

The term "antichrist" comes from John, the author of Revelation, but it appears in his first and second epistles, rather than in Revelation. According to I John 2:18, even first century believers had been told that the antichrist was coming, and that already many antichrists had arisen. In verse 22 of the same chapter, John provides a definition of the antichrist as "the liar…who denies that Jesus is the Christ." He is "the one who denies the Father and the Son." John reiterates this definition in 1 John 4:2-3, and then adds that the spirit of the antichrist is already in the world.

In John's second epistle, he identifies a critical activity of the antichrist when he writes in verse 7 that the antichrist is a deceiver. Thus, the antichrist has been identified for approximately 2,000 years as one who denies that Jesus came in the flesh; who denies that He is the Christ, the Messiah; who denies God the Father and God the Son; and whose hallmark activity will be deception. He is *anti* Christ in the sense that he is not only opposed to Jesus Christ, but he will also attempt to take His place as God.

B. Revelations from Daniel 2 and 7

An understanding of this critical character in the book of Revelation depends upon earlier revelations of the Lord to His prophets. Again, the framework of the prophecy is provided in the account of Daniel, who lived between 500 and 600 years before Christ.

The Lord had judged Judah for turning away from Him to idol worship and for turning away from His law. God Himself sent the Babylonians to judge His own people, and the Babylonians tore the Israelites from the land of Judah and destroyed the Temple and the cities. Most of the people of Judah, including Daniel and his companions, went into exile in Babylon for 70 years. Daniel and his companions were put in the service of King Nebuchadnezzar of Babylon. Shortly thereafter, chapter 2 recounts that King Nebuchadnezzar had dreams that troubled him. All his wise men were unable to tell him either the content or the interpretation of his dream. But Daniel and his companions prayed to God, and God gave Daniel both the content and the interpretation of the dream. Daniel returned to Nebuchadnezzar to tell him that there is a God in heaven who reveals mysteries, and he proceeded to relate the dream and its interpretation as God had given it to him.

Nebuchadnezzar had dreamed of a great statue that had terrified him. The head of the statue was made of fine gold, its breast and arms were made of silver, its belly and the upper thighs were made of bronze, its legs were made of iron, and its feet were made partly of iron and partly of clay. Then a stone that was cut out without hands struck the statue on its feet of iron and clay, and crushed not just the feet, but the entire statue. Then Daniel explained (in 2:44) that: "...in the days of those kings the God of heaven will set up a kingdom which will never be destroyed, and that kingdom will not be left for another people; it will crush and put an end to all these kingdoms, but it will itself endure forever."

Having told King Nebuchadnezzar what the king had dreamed, Daniel proceeded to the interpretation of the dream. The statue represented four earthly kingdoms, after which there would be another kingdom represented by the 10 toes, and it would be in the days of *those kings* – which, from the context, is a reference to the kingdom represented by the 10 toes, that God would put an end to all prior kingdoms and set up His own everlasting kingdom. Daniel told King Nebuchadnezzar that he, the king, represented the head of gold of the statue, but that his kingdom would come to an end and be replaced by the kingdom represented by the silver breast and arms of the statue. By the time Daniel was an elderly man, that next empire, the Medo-Persian Empire, represented by the breast and arms of silver of the statue of Nebuchadnezzar's dream, had conquered Babylon.

In Daniel 7, Daniel himself had either a dream or a vision of four beasts coming out of the sea. They are characterized as beasts because they represented kingdoms or world empires dominated by or controlled by Satan over the course of time; the common denominator in all these world empires was their persecution of the people of God, that is, Israel. Because Jesus Christ would come from that divinely chosen nation, and because the national salvation of Israel will, according to Romans 11, complete the spiritual kingdom of God, Satan has continually sought ways to destroy Israel in his vain attempt to frustrate Jesus Christ's rightful and sovereign rule over the earth.

The beasts of Daniel 7 correspond to the various metals of the statue of Nebuchadnezzar's dream in chapter 2; the first two earthly kingdoms represented were Babylon, and then Medo-Persia. The identity of the third kingdom is revealed in Daniel 8 as Greece, and then particularly Syria and Egypt as they fought over control of the territory of Israel. The identity of the fourth beast kingdom is not given in Scripture, but from secular history, most scholars conclude that this kingdom was Rome. This fourth kingdom was represented in Daniel 7 by a dreadful and terrifying beast (hereafter, the DT beast). Moreover, another kingdom, represented by the 10 horns on the DT beast, will, at some time that was future to Daniel and is still future, come out of the kingdom represented by the beast itself. Then another horn, a little one, will arise among them, and subdue three of the 10 horns. This little horn will wage war with the saints for 3½ years, and will overpower them. At the end of this time, judgment will come from the Ancient of Days, and then the Son of Man will be given dominion and glory and a kingdom. Daniel 7:14 tells us that His dominion is an everlasting dominion which will not pass away; and His kingdom is one which will not be destroyed. Clearly, there is a parallel between the 10 horns of chapter 7 and the 10 toes of chapter 2.

Beginning with Daniel 7:17, the interpretation of the four beasts begins. It is important to know that the words, "kings" and "kingdoms," are used interchangeably; they are synonyms. Although in verse 3 of chapter 7, Daniel says the beasts came *out of the sea*, at verse 17 Daniel is told that this means *from the earth*. Thus, these beasts arose from the mass of humanity, and were not of divine origin, although God is sovereign over all nations.

Daniel 7:23-26 contains a wealth of information about this fourth beast kingdom: The fourth beast would be a fourth kingdom on the earth, which would be different from all the other kingdoms, and it would devour the whole earth and tread it down and crush it. Because of the parallels to chapter 2, it is apparent that the fourth kingdom was Rome. As for the ten horns, <u>out of this kingdom</u> ten kings will arise in the future; and another will arise after them, and he will be different from the previous ones and will subdue three kings. This eleventh horn that arises after the first 10 is a reference to the antichrist, the ruler of the final beast empire in the last days. He will speak out against the Most High and wear down the saints of the Highest One, and he will intend to make alterations in times and in law; and they [meaning the saints] will be given into his hand for a time, times, and half a time – which means the same as 42 months, 1260 days, and 3½ years. But the court will sit for judgment, and his dominion will be taken away, annihilated and destroyed forever.

The fact that this eleventh horn, called the little horn in verse 8, uttered great boasts, is stated three times: in verse 8, in verse 11, and in verse 20. Verse 20 also describes this horn as being larger in appearance than its associates. How can this be reconciled with verse 8, which described the horn as little? Perhaps the reference to size has to do with relative power; the little horn begins relatively powerless because the 10 horns are the 10 kings who are ruling the earth, and he is not one of them. But then the little horn gains power as he uproots three of the kings, and gains ultimate power when all the kings transfer their power to him. By verse 21, the little horn has become quite powerful because the verse records that the little horn that is larger than its associates waged war with the saints and overpowered them.

Summary of information about the antichrist from Daniel 2 and 7:
In the years preceding the return of Christ, there will be a final kingdom that will rule over the whole world. It will be descended in some way from the ancient Roman Empire. This final kingdom will be ruled by 10 kings, represented by the 10 toes of Daniel 2, and by the 10 horns of Daniel 7. Another "horn," the antichrist, will arise from among them; thus, he is an eleventh. He will overthrow (pull out by the roots) three of the original 10 kings. He will grow in power to the point that all 10 kings will eventually cede their power to him, either voluntarily or because they have no choice.

This antichrist will boast; that means he will exalt and magnify himself. He will speak against God, and he will persecute the saints (Christians), and overpower them. God will allow him to overpower His followers for 3½ years. This, then, is a description of the Great Tribulation, which will begin at the midpoint of the final seven years, known as the 70th week of Daniel. But in His time, the Lord will come and the antichrist will be destroyed.

C. The beasts of Revelation 13 and 17

Revelation 13 describes what the devil (called the red dragon) and his antichrist (the first beast) and his false prophet (the second beast) will do during the Great Tribulation, that second 3½ year time period that is described as "a time, times, and half a time." The first beast has seven heads and 10 horns. The 10 horns on the beast represent the same 10 kings as the 10 horns of the DT beast of Daniel 7, and as the 10 toes of the statue of Daniel 2. This first beast of Revelation 13 also includes all of the beasts of Daniel 7; it is like a leopard, with feet like those of the bear, and with a mouth like that of a lion.

Revelation 13:2 relays information that is critical to understanding the character and motivations of the first beast: the dragon (the devil) will *give* the beast *his* power, *his* throne, and *his* authority. The timing of this investment of satanic power into the beast is at the midpoint of the 70th week; the purpose of this investment of power is so that the beast will carry out the devil's rage against Israel (the Jews) and Christians during that 3½ year time period known as "a time, times, and half a time."

There is yet another beast in Revelation 17. John records that he saw a woman sitting on a scarlet beast. Just like the *red dragon* (the devil, Satan) of Revelation 12 and the *beast that comes out of the sea* in Revelation 13, the *scarlet beast* of Revelation 17 has seven heads and 10 horns. Nevertheless, they represent only two beings, not three. The red dragon is Satan. The beast that comes out of the sea in Revelation 13 appears to be the same being as the scarlet beast of Revelation 17. In both chapters, the beast is a composite of all the beast empires seen in Daniel 7, as well as two empires that preceded the Babylonian Empire. Because those two empires were out of existence by the time that Daniel was given his vision, they did not relate to any future time relative to Daniel, and were therefore not included in his vision.

Summary: The first beast of Revelation 13 and the scarlet beast of Revelation 17 are the same beast, and that one beast represents Satan-inspired and Satan-controlled empires, both past and future, which persecuted and will persecute God's people.

The seven *heads* of the beast represent *past* beast kings and kingdoms. The 10 *horns* of the beast represent the *future* and final beast king and kingdom. They are the same future and final beast king and kingdom represented by the 10 horns of the DT beast of Daniel chapter 7, and by the 10 toes of the statue of Daniel 2.

D. The past beast kings and kingdoms represented by the seven heads of the beast

Revelation 17:9b-11 provides more information about the 7 heads:
The seven heads are seven mountains on which the woman sits, and they are seven kings; five have fallen, one is, the other has not yet come; and when he comes, he must remain a little while. And the beast which was and is not, is himself also an eighth, and is one of the seven, and he goes to destruction.

The seven heads represent seven different kings *and* their kingdoms that Satan has already used in his attempt to destroy God's chosen nation of Israel. The mountains in verse 9 represent kingdoms or empires. This interpretation comes from Daniel 2:35 and 44, in which a *mountain* that fills the whole earth is identified as the *kingdom* of Christ.

At the time that John wrote the book of Revelation, five of the beast empires were history, one was in existence at the time of his writing in approximately A.D. 90-95, and one was yet to come, although its existence would be brief. The eighth would come out of the first seven. Hindsight and history books reveal the identities of at least the first six beast empires.

The first five beast empires, which were already in the past from John's perspective, were:
1. Egypt, which enslaved the Israelites;
2. Assyria, which conquered the northern 10 tribes in 722 B.C.;
3. Babylon, which took the southern kingdom, including Daniel, into captivity for 70 years;
4. Medo-Persia, which held sway over the Israelites during the latter part of that 70 year captivity. The book of Esther is set in

that time, during which Haman tricked the king into issuing a decree to exterminate all the Jews in the kingdom;
5. Greece, in particular after Alexander the Great had died, and two of the four generals that divided up his territory fought over the land of Israel.

Those were the five that, according to Revelation 17:10, had fallen.

6. Rome was the empire that was in power at the time that John was writing the book of Revelation. It was Rome that sacked Jerusalem and destroyed the second Temple, killed millions of Jews, and scattered the rest across the world as the diaspora began in A.D. 70.

7. The seventh king and kingdom had not yet come as of the time that John was writing, but John was told that when that king came, he would remain a little while. This king and kingdom were not mentioned in Daniel 2 or 7.

8. Then the eighth king and kingdom would arise out of the seven.

There is not an exact correspondence of the seven heads or seven kings/kingdoms of Revelation 17 to the statue of Daniel 2 or to the four beasts of Daniel chapter 7, because those chapters of Daniel omit the first two empires mentioned in Revelation, focusing instead only on those empires which would dominate Israel and Jerusalem from Daniel's time forward. Moreover, there is no mention or even a hint of that seventh empire in Daniel 2 or 7. Yet Revelation 17 makes it clear that there is a seventh beast empire that appears *before* the eighth and final beast empire but *after* the Roman Empire. In other words, after the Roman Empire, which was the sixth beast empire in Revelation 17, but before the final 10 nation beast empire, which will be the eighth beast empire, there will be a seventh empire which is never even hinted at in the Old

Testament. Scholars and commentators opine that the omission is due to the fact that all that was revealed to Daniel were Gentile nations that would dominate Israel, or at least a remnant of Israel, only while she was on her way to, or remained in, or at least had free access to her own land, and in particular to the holy city of Jerusalem. The seventh beast empire is completely unlike the other prior six beast empires, because it would brutalize the people of Israel when they were *out of their land, dispersed* among the nations to the end of the earth.

The first scriptural reference to the seventh beast empire is in the book of Revelation, which was written in approximately A.D. 90-95, some 20 or so years after the diaspora had begun. There are several identifying characteristics of this seventh beast empire:

1. It must come after the sixth beast empire, which was Rome.

2. To qualify as a beast empire, it must persecute the Jewish people.

3. Revelation 17:10 says that "it must remain a little while."

4. It must exist and come to an end before Israel returned to her land in 1948. This is required because it had to be a nation that persecuted Israel while they were out of their land and dispersed among the nations. Since Israel returned to her land as a nation in 1948, the seventh beast empire must have existed sometime between A.D. 70 and 1948.

A few modern commentators have postulated that this seventh beast empire which persecuted the Jews was none other than the Third Reich of Adolf Hitler of Germany. Hitler repeatedly escaped attempted assassinations, in the most bizarre of circumstances. In addition, he was steeped in the occult and in satanic worship. Consistent with the requirement that "it must remain *a little while,*" the Third Reich was short-lived; most historians assign the years 1933 to 1945, which is only

12 years. In only the last 6 of those years (1939-1945), however, Germany took over, either by annexation or by military conquest, most of Europe.

Like all the six beast empires that preceded it, but with a single-minded obsession that exceeded theirs, Hitler's holocaust, his so-called "final solution," exterminated approximately six million Jews in a matter of only a few years, and this was at a time when Jews were scattered all over Europe, and furthermore, it was done without the benefit of all the technological advances since World War II that make it much harder to escape detection and detention and death. One distinction is that, unlike the prior six empires, Hitler's Reich never extended to the Holy Land. However, the fact that it did not reinforces its candidacy as the seventh beast empire, because control over the land of Israel would not be relevant or necessary while the Jews were scattered among the nations, away from their homeland.

Another candidate that has been proposed for the seventh beast empire is the Islamic/Turkish/Ottoman Empire, which began about A.D. 1300, and expanded to ultimately include much of southeast Europe, western Asia, and north Africa. The empire was dissolved in the aftermath of World War I. The Ottoman Empire lasted for approximately six centuries, however, and that seems inconsistent with the language of Revelation 17:10, which says this about the seventh king: "the other has not yet come; and when he comes, he must remain a little while." The Greek word used there is *oligos*, and it means puny, in extent, degree, number, duration or value. It is questionable whether the Ottoman Empire qualifies as puny, either in terms of duration, or of geographical extent. Nevertheless, it was an empire that existed between A.D. 70 and A.D. 1948.

Both Nazi Germany and the Ottoman Empire, however, occupied territory that was also encompassed within the Roman Empire. That may or may not be relevant. While it is clear that the *eighth* beast empire must be a form of revival of the Roman Empire, it is not clear whether the *seventh* must also be.

Comparison of Beast Empires

Revelation 17	Daniel 2 & 7
1. Egypt	Before Daniel's time
2. Assyria	Before Daniel's time
3. Babylon	1. Gold/lion
4. Medo-Persia	2. Silver/bear
5. Greece	3. Bronze/leopard
6. Rome	4. Iron/terrifying beast
7. Not yet come; remain a little while	not mentioned
8. 10 horns & beast	5. 10 horns & little horn

Summary: The *heads* of the beasts represent *past* kings and kingdoms. The identity of the seventh, which existed between A.D. 70 and A.D. 1948 is uncertain.

The *horns* represent the future and final eighth king and kingdom.

But—and here's where it gets confusing—the horns, the future eighth king and kingdom, will also be one of the seven heads, that is, one of the past seven kings or kingdoms. This characteristic comes from Revelation 17:11, which says: "And the beast which was and is not, is *himself* also an eighth, and *is one of the seven*, and he goes to destruction." Tying Daniel 7 back in, the leader of that eighth empire is also represented by the little horn that uproots three of the 10 horns of the DT beast, and then magnifies himself and rules over them all.

The little horn of Daniel 7 represents the antichrist. The ten horns represent his empire that will be world-wide. Both he and his empire will be "one of the seven," as well as the beast himself. Since the 10 horns grow out of the beast with the seven heads, that means that the eighth king/kingdom, the antichrist and his empire, will carry the DNA, so to speak, of the prior seven kings and kingdoms; he/it will be a composite of all the other beast empires of Satan that existed during Daniel's first 69 weeks and in the interlude that precedes the 70th week.

E. The eighth king (the antichrist) and his empire

Revelation 17:11 goes beyond saying that the eighth king comes from one of the prior seven beast empires; it declares that the eighth king *is* one of the prior seven. The text says: "the beast which *was and is not.*" In plain English, that means either a king or a kingdom used to exist – he or it "*was*" – but he or it no longer existed – "*it is not*" – as of the time John was writing in the first century. What the text appears to say is that the eighth king and kingdom will be that dead king or kingdom revived to life. Because the first beast of Revelation 13 is apparently the same as the beast of Revelation 17, parallel passages from chapter 13 may shed more light. In verse 3 of chapter 13, John reports that he saw one of the heads of the beast as if it had been slain, and his fatal wound was healed.

Since the seven heads of the beast represents both empires and their rulers, does the revival of one of the heads that was slain mean the revival of an empire or the revival of the ruler of a prior empire, or both? The answer is that, at a minimum, it means the revival of an empire. Daniel 7:7 says that the fourth beast, the DT beast, had 10 horns. These 10 horns constitute another (the eighth) beast empire. But why are they on the head of the fourth beast? Why isn't there just another whole beast? The reason is that the 10 horns of the DT beast of Daniel chapter 7 represent another empire coming *out of* that beast; they are, in a sense, an extension or a renewal or a revival in a different form. Therefore, the fatal wound on one of the seven heads of the beast, the wound that was healed, would represent a revival of that empire represented by the DT beast of Daniel chapter 7. Since the DT beast represented Rome, a logical conclusion is that the final, the eighth beast empire, will be a revived Roman Empire.

Does the revival of one of the heads that was slain refer to the revival of a *ruler* of a prior empire, as well as to the revival of the prior empire itself? It might.

Revelation 13:3 says that John saw one of the heads of the beast "as if it had been slain." This is the very same expression in Greek that is used to describe the Lamb in Revelation chapter 5, verse 6. In both cases the Greek word that is translated, "it had been slain" in 13:3, and simply as "slain" in 5:6 is *sphazo*, and it means "to butcher, especially an animal for food or in sacrifice; to slaughter." But in 13:3, it adds more after *sphazo*; it adds *thanatos*, which means death. So 13:3 says literally: "slaughtered or butchered *to death*."

In both Revelation 5:6 and 13:3, the English words, "as if" are the Greek word, *hos*, which means "in that manner." Chapter 13, verse 3 continues: "his fatal wound was healed." The Greek word for "fatal" is that same word, *thanatos*, death. Since the same Greek words for "as if slain" appear in both 5:6 and in 13:3, and since Jesus Christ literally died, then the logical conclusion is that the man who will be the antichrist also must have literally died at some point in the past. In verse 14 of this same chapter 13, the antichrist is described as the "beast who had the wound of the sword and has come to life."

Revelation 13:3-4 describes the reaction of the world: "And the whole earth was amazed and followed after the beast; and they worshiped the dragon, because he gave his authority to the beast; and they worshiped the beast, saying, 'Who is like the beast, and who is able to wage war with him?'" Their wonder and amazement is explained in Revelation 17:8, which says: "The beast that you saw *was and is not, and is about to come up out of the abyss* and to go to destruction. And those who dwell on the earth will wonder, whose name has not been written in the book of life from the foundation of the world, when they see the beast, that he *was and is not and will come*." Verse 11 repeats the same phrase: "And the beast which *was and is not*, is himself also an eighth, and is *one of the [prior] seven*, and he goes to destruction."

This sounds like science fiction! What these two passages, one out of Revelation 13, and the other out of Revelation 17, seem to be saying is that, not only has the ruler of this final beast empire lived and ruled before, but he will live and rule again. In order to deceive the world into believing that the antichrist is really the Christ, the antichrist must appear to "conquer death" just as Jesus Christ actually did. Unlike Jesus

Christ, however, whose resurrection conquered death so thoroughly that He will never die again, this antichrist, while literally raised from the dead—not "resurrected," but "raised" from the dead—by Satan, will die again. Revelation 17:8 says he will come up out of the abyss and will go to destruction. This restoration to life of a former leader of one of the past beast empires will be so astonishing that it should not be surprising that those who do not know the Bible will marvel and wonder and follow after the beast, and worship the dragon and worship the beast empowered by the dragon.

The world of unbelievers will be so enamored of this beast ruler who lived and died and lives again that they will believe he is invincible. Revelation 13:4 records their rhetorical question: "Who is like the beast, and who is able to wage war with him?" Obviously, these followers are not at war with him, so who is? The latter part of Daniel 11 indicates that there will be pockets of resistance to this world takeover by the antichrist. They need not be believers; they may just be people in power who don't want to cede their sovereignty to the antichrist. But Jews and believers in Jesus Christ will be the primary objects of his wrath and the targets of his technically advanced surveillance and weaponry.

As if one Satan-empowered beast ruling over the world were not bad enough, John reports in Revelation 13:11-12a: "And I saw *another* beast coming up out of the earth; and he had two horns like a lamb, and he spoke as a dragon. And he exercises all the authority of the first beast in his presence." Thus, the second beast is a spokesman for the first beast, the antichrist. Later, in Revelation 16:13, and thereafter, the second beast is called the false prophet. The remainder of Revelation 13:12 relays the frightening fact that the second beast, the false prophet, makes the world worship the first beast whose fatal wound was healed. Revelation 13:13 warns that the second beast will perform great signs. Remember that Jesus also warned, in Matthew 24:24, that "false Christs and false prophets will arise and will show great signs and wonders, so as to mislead/deceive, if possible, even the elect."

Revelation 13:11-17 lists the activities of this second beast:

1. He will exercise all the authority of the first beast in his presence. Is that significant? Does that mean that the second beast is unable to perform these miracles and signs and wonders when he is not in the presence of the first beast? The answer is unknown. What is known is that one of the great signs that he will perform is that he will make fire come down from heaven. It is almost as if he performs this particular sign to deceive the world, in particular the Jews, into believing that he is Elijah. They would be familiar with the account in I Kings 18 of Elijah's encounter with the 450 priests of Baal, and how Elijah called down fire from heaven to consume his offering. Unlike the ineffective priests of Baal, however, the false prophet, empowered by Satan, will succeed in accomplishing this sign.

2. The second beast will deceive those who dwell on the earth with the signs which he is able to perform in the presence of the first beast.

3. Having deceived those who dwell on the earth, the second beast will require them to make an image of the first beast who died and has come back to life.

4. Then the second beast will somehow give breath to the image of the first beast, so that the image can speak and cause those who do not worship the image of the beast to be killed.

5. Moreover, the second beast will cause everyone to be given the mark of the first beast on the right hand or on their forehead, without which one cannot buy or sell.

6. Verse 18, the last verse of Revelation 13, tells us that the number of the beast is that of a man, and his number is 6 6 6.

Summary: The eighth king and his empire will be the antichrist and his world-wide empire. It will begin with 10 kings (the 10 horns), and then the antichrist will overthrow three of them. This empire will be in some form a revived Roman Empire. This does not necessarily mean Roman, as in Italian, as in Western European, because the Roman Empire comprised all the territory that encompasses the Mediterranean Sea.

The text of Revelation 17 seems to be saying that the antichrist himself will be a ruler of one of the prior seven beast empires. Apparently, the Lord will, in His sovereignty, allow Satan to raise from the dead that prior ruler, and then Satan (the red dragon) will infuse this person with his power and authority. The antichrist will certainly be Satan-inspired, and possibly Satan-possessed. He will rule over the whole world and his rule will be enforced by his false prophet.

F. Further insights from Daniel 11:36 and following

Chapters 10, 11, and 12 of the book of Daniel are all one event that Daniel experienced in the third year of Cyrus the Persian. This was near the end of the time of the 70-year captivity, and Daniel was by this time an elderly man.

The entire content of chapter 10 constitutes an introduction to the revelation contained in chapters 11 and 12. Chapter 11 is divided into 2 major divisions: (1) the first consists of 11:2-35, and it deals with the immediate future, from Daniel's time to Antiochus Ephiphanes (this subject is covered in Section H of chapter 3 of this book); (2) the second, 11:36 through 12:4, deals with the far future, the end times just before the second advent of Christ.

Daniel 11:35 is the transition verse from the first passage about the first, "prototype" antichrist, to the end of days, when the ultimate antichrist will rule the world. This verse says: "And some of those who have insight will fall, in order to refine, purge, and make them pure, *until the end time*; because it is still to come at the appointed time."

Times of persecution refine, purge, and purify, and this purging process of God's people that began thousands of years ago will continue until the time of the end. The mention of "the end time" in verse 35 is notice that, from verse 36 on, the prophecy leaps over the intervening centuries to the time of the 10 toes of the statue of Daniel 2, to the time of the 10 horns and the little horn of Daniel 7, and to the time of the prince who is to come of Daniel 9. Beginning in verse 36, prophecy is unfolded that is as yet unfulfilled, about the king of the last kingdom before God sets up His eternal kingdom; it will be the last kingdom to rule Daniel's people before God's just judgment comes. This is the kingdom of the antichrist.

Daniel chapter 11:36-45 describes that person and his activities directly, but they are enigmatic. Verse 36 says, in pertinent part: "Then ['then' meaning at the end time referred to in the preceding verse 35] the king will do as he pleases, and he will **exalt and magnify himself above every god, and will speak monstrous things against the God of gods…**"

These descriptions of the antichrist exalting himself and magnifying himself and speaking monstrous things against the God of gods are consistent with the following other passages, some of which have been mentioned before in this book:

> *While I was contemplating the horns, behold, another horn, a little one, came up among them, and three of the first horns were pulled out by the roots before it; and behold, this horn possessed eyes like the eyes of a man, and* **a mouth uttering great boasts.** *(Daniel 7:8)*

> *Then I kept looking because of* **the sound of the boastful words which the horn was speaking…** *(Daniel 7:11)*

> *…the other horn which came up, and before which three of them fell, namely, that horn which had eyes and* **a mouth uttering great boasts,** *and which was larger in appearance than its associates. I*

*kept looking, and that horn was **waging war with the saints** [the children of God] **and overpowering them.** (Daniel 7:20-21)*

*And **he will speak out against the Most High and wear down the saints of the Highest One**, and he will intend to make alterations in times and in law; and they will be given into his hand for a time, times, and half a time. (Daniel 7:25)*

*And there was given to him **a mouth speaking arrogant words and blasphemies;** and authority to act for forty-two months was given to him. And **he opened his mouth in blasphemies against God, to blaspheme His name and His tabernacle, that is, those who dwell in heaven.** And **it was given to him to make war with the saints and to overcome them;** and authority over every tribe and people and tongue and nation was given to him. (Revelation 13:5-7)*

*And he [the second beast, the false prophet] **makes the earth and those who dwell in it to worship the first beast.** (Revelation 13:12)*

*…the man of lawlessness is revealed, the son of destruction, **who opposes and exalts himself above every so-called god or object of worship, so that he takes his seat in the Temple of God, displaying himself as being God.** (II Thessalonians 2:3b-4)*

What is abundantly plain from Daniel 11:36 and the accompanying cross references is that this antichrist will be permitted by God to prosper and to have authority over the world for a period of time variously known as "a time, times, and half a time," and as 42 months, and as 1260 days, and as 3½ years. This time period will be the latter half of Daniel's 70th week, during which he will not only blaspheme against the true God, the great I AM, but he will also exalt himself as God, and demand that the world worship him as God. That act, setting himself up as God and demanding the world's worship, will be the abomination of desolation of Daniel 9:27, referred to by Jesus in Matthew 24:15. This will occur at the midpoint of the 70th week. Having been fully revealed as the man of lawlessness, the antichrist will viciously persecute all of God's people, who refuse to worship him.

The next verse of Daniel 11 (verse 37) says that he, the antichrist, will show no regard for the gods of his fathers. Some English translations say, "God of his fathers," instead of "gods of his fathers." It is not clear which meaning is intended. If it is "gods," then it is likely that the antichrist will be a Gentile, meaning not a Jew. If it is "God," then he will be a Jew. The Hebrew word used there is *elohim*, which can mean either "gods" or the triune God. It is important to note, however, that elsewhere, when Daniel means the triune God, he uses the word, *Jehovah*, not *elohim*. Moreover, since Revelation 17:11 says that the eighth and final beast empire will arise out of the prior seven empires, it, too, will attempt to destroy the Jewish people. Therefore, it stands to reason that the head of this empire would also be a Gentile.

The problem with this conclusion is, of course, that the Jews have always looked for a Messiah coming from within themselves; therefore, it seems highly unlikely that they would ever acknowledge a Gentile as Messiah. But the forked tongue of the false prophet will be so impressively *deceptive* and so powerfully persuasive that "many," to borrow Daniel's term, will willingly enter into a covenant with the antichrist. Moreover, most of the world, whether Jew or Gentile, will ride on the tide of popularity and political correctness and will obey the command of the second beast (the false prophet) to worship the first beast (the antichrist). Remember that Jesus warned in Matthew 24:24 that false Christs and false prophets would arise and would show great signs and wonders, so great that, if possible, it would mislead or deceive even the elect.

This same verse, Daniel 11:37, says that the antichrist will also show no regard for the desire of women. The phrase that is translated as "desire of women" has been the subject of much speculation. There are several possibilities. One is that, if the antichrist is Jewish, it could be alluding to the desire of every Jewish woman to be the mother of the Messiah. Another is that he will not be attracted to women. Yet another is that it is a reference to the cult of Tammuz (Adonis), the queen of heaven, whose cult was popular for centuries. References to the queen of heaven appear in Jeremiah 7:18, and 44:17-19, 25. This same idol goddess is called Tammuz in Ezekiel 8:14.

Daniel 11:38 adds that the antichrist will honor a god of fortresses or of forces. The context demands that the meaning be a lower case "god," because the antichrist would never honor God, the great I AM. This verse is relatively clear: the antichrist will show disrespect or contempt for all other gods, but will honor this "god of forces," or "god of fortresses" alone – while still demanding that the world acknowledge him as God. Not only will he blaspheme against God by rejecting Him as well as all false gods, but he will also blaspheme against God by claiming to be God himself. Nevertheless, he will honor a god of forces or fortresses, which may be the same as the foreign god of the next verse, verse 39, which states that he will take action against the strongest of fortresses with the help of a foreign god. It is likely that the foreign god, this god of force or god of fortresses, is none other than Satan. After all, Revelation 13 says that Satan invests the first beast – that is, antichrist – with his own power, throne, and authority, so it would be logical for the antichrist to be relying on Satan's power to accomplish his goals.

In these verses of Daniel 11, the antichrist is pictured as an absolute ruler, but there are other cross-references from Revelation which also indicate the existence of a one-world government at this time:

> *And it was given to him to make war with the saints and to overcome them; and authority over* **every tribe and people and tongue and nation** *was given to him. (Revelation 13:7)*

> *And he [the second beast] exercises all the authority of the first beast in his presence. And he* **makes the earth and those who**

dwell in it to worship the first beast, whose fatal wound was healed. *(Revelation 13:12)*

He [the second beast] *causes* **all, the small and the great, and the rich and the poor, and the free men and the slaves,** *to be given a mark on their right hand, or on their forehead, and he provides that* **no one** *should be able to buy or to sell,* **except the one who has the mark,** *either the name of the beast or the number of his name. (Revelation 13:16-17)*

And the ten horns which you saw are ten kings, who have not yet received a kingdom, but **they receive authority as kings with the beast** *for one hour. These have one purpose and* **they give their power and authority to the beast.** *(Revelation 17:12-13)*

These verses make it clear that, not only will there be one world government, but there will also be one world economy – and it will all be under the power and authority of the beast who is the antichrist.

The battles described at the end of Daniel 11 seem to be a form of rebellion against the antichrist, and indicate an attempt either to prevent the formation of his one world government or, if it is already formed, to break it up.

The "end time" that was mentioned in Daniel 11:35 appears again in verse 40 to make it clear that the military struggle described here is one which will characterize *the end of the age*. The king of verses 36-39 (the antichrist) will be attacked by the king of the south and the king of the north. These kings of the north and the south are different from the kings described earlier in chapter 11; those kings and the battles described *there* were fulfilled historically. The warfare described here at *the end* of chapter 11 does not match anything in history.

Summary: The antichrist will exalt himself above all false gods and above the true God, the great I AM. He will demand that the entire world worship him as God. He will move to quash any rebellion against his growing power. Aided and enabled by the power of Satan, and permitted by God to thrive, he will be given authority over the entire world, and he will wage war against all Jews and Christians for the latter half of the 70th week; indeed, he will come very close to his goal of annihilating every last one of them. There will be one world economy, one world government, and one world religion.

G. Clues to the origin or ethnicity of the antichrist from Daniel 9:26

Daniel 9:26 says: "[T]he people of *the prince who is to come* will destroy the city and the sanctuary." "The prince who is to come" is a reference to the antichrist. He will come from the people who destroyed the city of Jerusalem and the Temple of God. History records that it was the Romans who sacked Jerusalem and destroyed the Temple in A.D. 70.

In addition, the fourth beast of Daniel 7 represents the Roman Empire, and the 10 horns which represent the final beast empire come out of that beast, along with the eleventh horn which represents the antichrist. Similarly, the iron legs of the statue of Daniel 2 represent the Roman Empire and the 10 toes of iron and clay are the parallel of the 10 horns of chapter 7, representing the future and final beast empire.

Other facts gleaned from Daniel 2 about this final kingdom of 10 kings are these:

1. The iron and the clay mixed together represent a divided kingdom, one that is part strong and part brittle. (Daniel 2:41-42)

2. The kings will not adhere to one another, even as iron does not combine with pottery. (Daniel 2:43)

The beginning of verse 43 adds an additional fact, but its meaning is most obscure. It says that: "And in that you saw the iron mixed with common clay, they will combine with one another in the seed of men."

Perhaps this is describing a mix of numerous races and cultures. The 10 horns of Daniel 7, as well as the 10 toes of Daniel 2 represent 10 kingdoms or kings which will be loosely united in a federation. Possibly they will be so diverse and different from one another that there cannot be any real unity. Clearly, this is yet future because there has never been in the history of man 10 kingdoms loosely federated together and yet looked upon as one kingdom.

One other significant fact comes from Daniel 2:34-35; it is that, while the stone struck the statue on its feet with 10 toes, the rest of the statue was crushed at the same time. If the rest of the statue represents past kingdoms, how is it that they are crushed at the same time as the feet and toes? The answer to that question is a clue to the makeup of the final beast empire and the identity of the antichrist.

The fact that the entire statue was crushed at the same time indicates that *all four* of the prior empires, not just Rome, must be present in some form at the time of the end. The final kingdom will be composed of all four of the earlier empires: Babylon, Medo-Persia, Greece, as well as Rome. How is that possible? The answer is that the territory encompassed by the past beast empires represented by the statue of Daniel 2 and by the beasts of Daniel 7 (not including the two beast empires that existed before the time of Daniel: Egypt and Assyria) was very similar. While some of the empires drove further into Asia and others drove further into Europe, all involved the territory of the Middle East.

When the Babylonians were conquered by the Medes and the Persians, that may have been the end of the Babylonian empire, but it was not the end of those people groups. It was the same when the Greeks overcame Persia, and the Romans overcame the Seleucids and the Ptolemies. The people of any particular area in the Middle East may have been subject to one empire, and then to another, but they continued to propagate after their own kind. This, then, may be how the statue of Daniel chapter 2 could be crushed in its entirety when the stone, representing Jesus Christ, strikes the statue at its feet. The final beast empire will be a composite of, it will have elements of, all the preceding empires, because they all covered most of the same territory in the Middle East.

Another important fact to observe is that Daniel 9:26 says: "the *people*" of the prince who is to come. It does not say: "the *nation*" of the prince who is to come. The Hebrew word for "nations" would have been *goy*, which implies a territorial or governmental unity identity. The Hebrew word for people is *am*, which implies familial or tribal ties based on relationship or common ancestry. The "prince who is to come" is the antichrist, and this verse reveals that he will be descended from the people who destroyed Jerusalem and the Temple. Another way of saying this is that the people who destroyed the city and the sanctuary will be the ancestors of the antichrist. The next logical question is, who *were* the people who destroyed Jerusalem and the Temple?

The Emperor of Rome at the time was Vespasian, and he chose his son Titus to lead the Eastern Legions of the Roman empire. In the campaign against Judea, Titus led the Fifth and Tenth Legions, and met with his father, who had the Fifteenth Legion with him. Some sources say there were three other legions as well, for a total of six. But it was primarily the Tenth Legion that actually breached the walls of the city, and then destroyed the Temple. While the Roman soldiers were Roman citizens, ethnically they were Arabs, Syrians, Turks, and Persians. The Tenth Legion, in particular, was made up of soldiers from Turkey and from Syria; this Legion was garrisoned near Antioch, on the border between Syria and Turkey.

Those who believe that the seventh beast empire of Revelation 17 was the Ottoman Empire conclude that it (the Ottoman Empire) is the beast empire that will be revived, with the 10 nations (the 10 horns, the 10 toes) being the various Muslim countries that surround Israel. The one-world religion will be Islam, and the antichrist will come out of Turkey. Since the eighth and final beast empire must be a revival of the Roman Empire, it is important to remember that the Ottoman empire covered some of the same land as the Roman Empire, in particular the Middle East.

If the seventh beast empire was Nazi Germany instead of the Ottoman Empire, then the revived eighth empire will also arise from lands that were included in the Roman Empire. The difference, however, is that Nazi Germany never extended its reach to the Middle East.

Another possible country of origin of the antichrist would be Syria, just to the south of Turkey, particularly in view of the fact that the Old Testament prototype of the antichrist was Antiochus Epiphanes, who ruled over Syria in the inter-testamental period. It was he who committed the first abomination of desolation in the Temple in Jerusalem in approximately 168 B.C.

Summary: Most Christians were taught that the antichrist would be European, and, while he may be, other possibilities should be considered, based on these facts:

1. In Daniel 2, the stone crushed not just the feet and toes of the statue, but the entire statue all at the same time.

2. When Daniel had the vision of the four beasts coming out of the sea in chapter 7, it is possible to infer that they all came out together, at the same time, because Daniel says that they were all different from one another. That might indicate a connection between them as well.

3. Although their borders differed, the heart of the territory encompassed by the four empires (Babylon, Medo-Persia, Greece, and Rome) was the same.

4. All the modern nations within those territories, with the exception of Israel, are Muslim today.

H. Forerunner/prototype in Antiochus Epiphanes

Jesus said, in Matthew 24:15: "Therefore when you see the abomination of desolation which was spoken of through Daniel the prophet, standing in the holy place (let the reader understand)…" Since Daniel 9 has been covered in the preceding sections of this book, the reader of this book *would* understand the reference to Daniel. The original listeners, the disciples of Jesus, would also have studied the writings of the prophet Daniel, and would have the same understanding. But they had an even fuller understanding than most of today's readers because they were familiar with a part of Israel's history that is not recorded in the Bible; portions relating to that time in their history are recorded in some of the books of the Apocrypha, most notably in the books of the Maccabees. As a result of their familiarity with their own history, they would have immediately understood the reference to the abomination of desolation.

The original "abomination of desolation" was committed in the Temple (the second Temple, which had been rebuilt after the Babylonian exile) in approximately 168 B.C. by a Syrian leader named Antiochus Epiphanes. This was a little under 200 years prior to the time that Jesus made the reference to it. The point is that the Jews of Jesus' time knew of this tyrant and of his atrocities against the Jews.

The coming of Antiochus Epiphanes was also foretold by Daniel, approximately 400 years before he entered the world's stage. This prophecy is in Daniel 8 and in 11:21-34. Because he was a prototype, a foreshadowing, of the antichrist of the very end times, a brief examination of Daniel 8 and the passage in Daniel 11 is worthwhile.

The vision that is recorded in chapter 8 was given to Daniel toward the end of his life, about a decade before the Babylonian Empire was conquered by the Medo-Persian Empire. In his vision, Daniel saw a ram and a goat. The ram represented the Medo-Persian Empire that would soon conquer the Babylonian Empire, and the goat represented Greece.

(*See* verses 20 and 21 of chapter 8.) The large horn on the goat represented Alexander the Great.

DANIEL 8:

> ⁸*Then the male goat magnified himself exceedingly. But as soon as he was mighty, the large horn was broken; and in its place there came up four conspicuous horns toward the four winds of heaven.* ⁹*And out of one of them came forth a rather small horn which grew exceedingly great toward the south, toward the east, and toward the Beautiful Land* [which means the land of Israel].

After the death of Alexander at the young age of 32 or 33, his empire was eventually divided among four of his generals (the four conspicuous horns of verse 8). Cassander and Lysimachus (by the way, this general was also known by the name Antigonus) are not relevant to any further portion of this prophecy, because their geographical areas of power and influence did not cover any of the land of Israel, and politically they did not interact with it. The other two, Seleucus, and Ptolemy, are the subjects of the remainder of this particular prophecy. They engaged in an extended tug-of-war over the land of Israel, a subject which is covered in great detail in the first 35 verses of chapter 11 of Daniel. The "rather small horn" which came out of one of the four horns of the goat came out of the Seleucid dynasty.

CONTINUING IN DANIEL 8:

> ¹⁰*And it* [meaning the "rather small horn"] *grew up to the host of heaven and caused some of the host and some of the stars to fall to the earth, and it trampled them down.* ¹¹*It even magnified itself to be equal with the Commander of the host; and it removed the regular sacrifice from Him, and the place of His sanctuary was thrown down.* ¹²*And on account of transgression the host will be given over to the horn along with the regular sacrifice; and it will fling truth to the ground and perform its will and prosper.* ¹³*Then I heard a holy*

one speaking, and another holy one said to that particular one who was speaking, "How long will the vision about the regular sacrifice apply, while the transgression causes horror, so as to allow both the holy place and the host to be trampled?" ¹⁴And he said to me, "For 2,300 evenings and mornings; then the holy place will be properly restored."

These verses 10-14 require some explanation. The host refers to the holy people that belong to God, and the stars are leaders among the holy people. God Almighty is the Commander of the host. Verse 11 tells us that this rather small horn magnified himself to be equal with God, and he, that is, the rather small horn, stopped the regular sacrifices in the Temple and somehow threw down the sanctuary. Verse 12 tells us that, on account of transgression, which means because of the ongoing disobedience of the Jewish people, the Jews would be given over to the power of the rather small horn. Verses 13 and 14 tell us that the time period that both the holy place and the Jews would be trampled would be 2,300 evenings and mornings.

While the activities of this rather small horn appear to be very similar to that of the little horn of Daniel 7, particularly their persecution of the Jews and the stopping of the sacrifices in the Temple, they do *not* represent the same person. They represent different people in different time periods and from different empires. Here are some of the prominent differences:

1. This "rather small horn" of Daniel 8 comes out of the remains of the *Greek Empire*. In contrast, the "little horn" of Daniel 7 comes up among the 10 horns of the beast which represents the *Roman Empire*.

2. The 10 horns and the eleventh little horn of Daniel 7 represent a still-future kingdom and king. Chapter 8 describes an empire

that, while future from Daniel's perspective, is past from our perspective.

3. The little horn of Daniel 7 is an eleventh horn that comes up among the original 10 and uproots three of those original 10. In contrast, the rather small horn of Daniel 8 is a fifth horn that comes out of one of the original four.

4. The little horn of Daniel 7 persecutes God's people for a period of time known as "a time, times, and half a time," also known as 1260 days, also known as 42 months, and also known as 3½ years. The rather small horn of Daniel 8 also persecutes God's people, but the time period given there is 2,300 evenings and mornings.

5. The little horn of Daniel 7 represents the antichrist of the very end times; but the rather small horn of Daniel 8 represents a historical figure from our perspective, Antiochus Epiphanes. As the interpretation of Daniel's vision of chapter 8 is given to him, more details are provided about Antiochus Epiphanes, beginning in verse 22:

> *²²And the broken horn and the four horns that arose in its place represent four kingdoms which will arise from his nation, although not with his power. ²³And in the latter period of their rule, when the transgressors have run their course, a king will arise insolent and skilled in intrigue. ²⁴And his power will be mighty, but not by his own power, and he will destroy to an extraordinary degree and prosper and perform his will; he will destroy mighty men and the holy people. ²⁵And through his shrewdness he will cause deceit to succeed by his influence; and he will magnify himself in his heart, and he will destroy many while they are at*

ease. He will even oppose the Prince of princes, but he will be broken without human agency.

This insolent king is the same as the rather small horn that arises from one of the four horns of the goat. Antiochus Epiphanes was a prototype, a forerunner, of the ultimate antichrist who will come on the scene prior to the second coming of Christ. Antiochus Epiphanes was the eighth king of the Syrian dynasty, also known as the Seleucid Empire, and he reigned from 175 B.C. until his death in 164 B.C.. Verse 11 of chapter 8 says that this rather small horn (Antiochus Epiphanes) even magnified itself/himself to be equal with the Commander of the host, which means he thought he was a god, and demanded to be treated as such. He had coins minted with the inscription, *Theos Epiphanes*, which means "God manifest." Antiochus liked to be called *Epiphanes* but his enemies, the Jews, used a play on words giving him another name, *Epimanes*, which means "Madman."

His persecution of the Jews began, depending upon the source consulted, between 171 and 168 B.C. He sent his men into the Jewish Temple and stopped the twice-daily regular sacrifices. Instead, he had a pig (an unclean animal to the Jews) sacrificed on the altar. Then he had a statue of Zeus erected in the Holy of Holies. The ark of the covenant was no longer there because it had disappeared during the Babylonian captivity.

The first 35 verses of Daniel chapter 11 have been fulfilled in history. The passage that begins at verse 21 delineates the activity of this rather small horn, Antiochus Epiphanes, who is characterized in this chapter as a "despicable person." Verse 31 describes the first abomination of desolation: "And forces from him will arise, desecrate the sanctuary fortress, and do away with the regular sacrifice. And they will set up the abomination of desolation." Verse 32 continues: "And by smooth words he will turn to godlessness those who act wickedly toward the covenant, but the people who know their God will display strength and take action."

Thus, when Jesus spoke of an abomination of desolation in Matthew 24:15, his listeners not only understood the reference to Daniel (in portions of what we know as chapters 8, 9, and 11), but they also knew of the first abomination that had desolated the Temple fewer than 200 years earlier.

Summary: Daniel 8 describes Daniel's vision regarding two empires that were future from Daniel's perspective, Medo-Persia, and Greece. Beginning with Cyrus the Persian, the Israelites were allowed to return to Israel and to rebuild Jerusalem and the Temple. But under the Greeks, and particularly under the domination of Antiochus Epiphanes, the rather small horn who arose out of one of the four divisions of the Greek Empire, the city of Jerusalem and the Temple were again desolated. Daniel was given this vision in about 551 B.C. and its fulfillment in the time period between 171 B.C. and 165 B.C. was still future relative to him. There is an obvious parallel, however, between the cessation of the daily sacrifices by Antiochus Epiphanes and the coming interruption of the daily sacrifices by the future antichrist which will occur 3½ years before the second coming of Christ.

I. The end of the antichrist

The Lord will bring this lawless one to an end by the appearance of His coming. II Thessalonians 2:8 states: "And then that lawless one will be revealed whom *the Lord will slay with the breath of His mouth* and *bring to an end by the appearance of His coming...*" At first glance, it may appear that Paul is saying the same thing in two different ways when he says, in this verse 8, that the Lord will slay this lawless one with the breath of His mouth *and* the Lord will bring this lawless one to an end by the appearance of His coming. But actually Paul is describing two different things.

The Greek word that is translated into English as "bring to an end" means to render inoperative, to render useless, to make of no effect.

When the Lord Jesus appears with the clouds to gather together His own and to begin His Day of the Lord judgment, He will render the antichrist powerless, inoperative, impotent, and useless. The antichrist will remain on his throne until the end of Daniel's 70th week, but, once the Day of the Lord begins, the Lord alone will be exalted. The antichrist's powers will be limited to the ability to summon the nations together for the battle of Armageddon. And there, the Lord will slay the lawless one with the breath of His mouth. The Greek word for "slay" means to take up, to take away violently, to abolish, to put to death, to murder, to slay. Revelation 19:19-21 describes the end of the antichrist:

> *^{19}And I saw the beast* [the antichrist] *and the kings of the earth and their armies, assembled to make war against Him who sat upon the horse, and against His army. ^{20}And the beast was seized, and with him the false prophet who performed the signs in his presence, by which he deceived those who had received the mark of the beast and those who worshiped his image; these two were thrown alive into the lake of fire which burns with brimstone. ^{21}And the rest were killed with the sword which came from the mouth of Him who sat upon the horse, and all the birds were filled with their flesh.*

Summary: Once the Day of the Lord begins, the Sovereign Lord will allow the antichrist to remain on his throne for whatever remains of the second half of the 70th week, but he will be powerless to do anything beyond gathering the nations under his command to the place which in Hebrew is called Har-Magedon. In the Day of the Lord, the Lord alone will be exalted. The antichrist and his false prophet will be seized and thrown alive into the lake of fire to be tormented forever.

• 4 •

WHAT IS THE RAPTURE AND WHEN IS IT?

A. Biblical descriptions of the rapture

Like the doctrine of the Trinity, the rapture is a Biblical doctrine which is never called by its name in the Bible. We get the word "rapture" from the Latin translation of the Bible commonly known as the Vulgate. St. Jerome is credited with having accomplished this translation from the original Hebrew and Greek in about A.D. 400. In the Latin Vulgate, the word that appears in many English translations as "caught up" or "taken away" was the Latin verb "rapere" (noun: "raptus") and it is from the Latin word that we get the English word "rapture." The original *Greek* word used by Paul in I Thessalonians 4:17 was "harpazo." The verb, both in Greek and in Latin, means to seize upon with force, to snatch out or away, to carry off speedily.

According to the Bible, what happens at the time of this event which is popularly known today as the rapture? Paul's first letter to the Thessalonians describes it well. In this letter, Paul was answering the question: what happens to believers when the Lord comes again? There are really two parts to that question. The first part is: what happens to believers who have already died – that is, they died or will die before He returns? When a believer dies, his spirit/soul (for the purposes of this book, these words are used interchangeably) separates from his physical body and goes immediately into the presence of Christ, but his body, in an appearance of sleep, decays and disintegrates. Thus, the first part of the question really is: what will happen to the dust that the bodies of dead believers disintegrated into when Christ returns? And the second part is: what happens to the believers who are still alive at the time of His return?

In I Thessalonians 4:14, Paul assured the Thessalonians, and all believers since that time, that, because Jesus died and was resurrected, God will bring those who have fallen asleep in Jesus with Him when He comes. This means that the spirits of those who have died in Christ will come with Christ because they, their spirits, are always with Him.

I Thessalonians 4:16-17 are two of the most exciting and comforting verses in the Bible. Verse 16 begins: "For the Lord Himself will descend from heaven with a shout, with the voice of the archangel, and with the trumpet of God…" It is the Lord Himself who will descend. Not an angel or an emissary or messenger, but Jesus Christ Himself. The very same Jesus whose ascension into heaven was described in Acts 1. And His coming will be announced to the entire world with a shout of authority, the voice of the archangel, and the trumpet call of victory. I Thessalonians 4:16 concludes: "… and the dead in Christ shall rise first." In this statement, Paul specifically addresses the concern of the Thessalonians: that when Jesus returned, He would rapture the living but leave the dead Christians in their graves. But Paul clarifies that they will even precede those who are alive and remaining on the earth at the time that Jesus returns.

Observation of the text is very important here. Verse 16 says: "the dead *in Christ* shall rise first." This is a resurrection of believers only. The unsaved dead are left in their graves to be raised for judgment at the end of the millennium. But *all* the believers in Christ shall be raised. This includes the Old Testament saints, both named and unnamed in Hebrews chapter 11. It includes the apostles who died 2000 years ago. It includes the great men of the faith, like Martin Luther, the Wesley brothers, Charles Spurgeon, Martyn Lloyd-Jones, C. S. Lewis. It includes people we knew personally, people we loved, who were believers in Christ. And, if we die *in Christ* before He returns, we, too, will be among those.

I Thessalonians 4:17 declares: "Then we who are alive and remain shall be caught up together with them in the clouds to meet the Lord in the air, and thus we shall always be with the Lord." That verse really says three things about those believers who are alive on the earth when Jesus comes again. First, believers will be reunited in the clouds with the dead in Christ who have come with Him. Second, believers will meet the Lord in the air. And third, believers, whether the dead in Christ or those who are alive and remain, will always be with the Lord thereafter. What a wonderful verse!

Paul also describes the rapture in his *second* letter to the Thessalonians. Chapter 2, verse 1 says: "Now we request you, brethren, with regard to the coming of our Lord Jesus Christ, and our gathering together to Him..." Although different words are used in Greek and in English, the "gathering together to Him" is, like "caught up," also a description of the rapture.

Summary: According to the Bible, the rapture is the physical resurrection of both the living and the dead *in Christ*, at which time all believers will be caught up into the presence of Christ.

B. Spiritual bodies

Since all believers will be resurrected in the rapture, what will their resurrected bodies be like, of those who have already died, and of those who are raptured alive?

All human beings, including Jesus Christ during His incarnation, had or have a physical body which experiences death, which is the separation of the spirit from the body. But at the resurrection, first of Christ, and later of the rest of His followers, there will be a spiritual body. A "spiritual body" may sound like an oxymoron because most people tend to think of "spiritual" as the opposite of "physical." A quick review of

I Corinthians 15:35-58 dispels that notion. Selected verses beginning at verse 42 will suffice to make the point.

I Corinthians 15

> ⁴²*So also is the resurrection of the dead. It is sown a perishable body, it is raised an imperishable body;* ⁴⁴*it is sown a natural body, it is raised a spiritual body. If there is a natural body, there is also a spiritual body.* ⁴⁶*However, the spiritual is not first, but the natural; then the spiritual.* ⁴⁷*The first man is from the earth, earthy; the second man is from heaven.* ⁴⁹*And just as we have borne the image of the earthy, we shall also bear the image of the heavenly.* ⁵⁰*Now I say this, brethren, that flesh and blood cannot inherit the kingdom of God; nor does the perishable inherit the imperishable.* ⁵¹*Behold, I tell you a mystery; we shall not all sleep* [in this context, "sleep" clearly refers to the death of a believer], *but we shall all be changed,* ⁵²*in a moment, in the twinkling of an eye, at the last trumpet; for the trumpet will sound, and the dead will be raised imperishable, and we shall be changed.* [Doesn't this verse sound a lot like I Thessalonians 4:16-17?] ⁵³*For this perishable must put on the imperishable, and this mortal must put on immortality.* ⁵⁴*But when this perishable will have put on the imperishable, and this mortal will have put on immortality, then will come about the saying that is written, "Death is swallowed up in victory."*

The spiritual bodies, which some also call the resurrection bodies, will be suited for the eternal realm. They will be real, physical bodies, similar to that of Jesus Christ after His resurrection. And these new resurrection bodies will reflect the life of Christ, because they will be free from the curse which all natural bodies are now subject to. Somehow God will collect all the molecules and building blocks that once constituted the dead believers' bodies and He will raise indestructible brand-new bodies, clothed with immortality, healed, and restored, raised to live forever, never to die again. These resurrection bodies will be reunited with their spirits who came with the Lord. Then the bodies of those who are still alive and on earth at the time of the rapture will also be changed in that twinkling of the eye into resurrection bodies.

Summary: Here is the chronology of I Thessalonians 4:13-18, together with I Corinthians 15:51-54:

First, Jesus Christ died and rose again. In the intervening millennia since His resurrection and ascension, believers have died, which means that their bodies and spirits were separated. Their bodies were buried, or lost at sea, or destroyed by fire; by one means or another, those bodies decayed and decomposed. In contrast to their bodies, their spirits went immediately upon their death to be at home in the presence of the Lord.

Not all Christians will die, however, before Jesus Christ returns; some will be alive when He returns. At that time, the Lord Himself will descend from heaven. His coming will be announced with a shout, the voice of the archangel, and with the trumpet of God. Then the reconstituted immortal bodies of dead believers will be resurrected as their spirits come with Christ. Somehow Christ will give these spirits their resurrection bodies at this time.

Then believers who are still alive on earth will be caught up in the air to meet with the Lord. In the process, their mortal, perishable bodies, which have been subject to the curse, will be changed into immortal, imperishable bodies in the twinkling of an eye. These living believers will also be reunited with those spirits who have come with the Lord and have just received their resurrection bodies. Thereafter, all believers, both the living and the formerly dead, will be with Him always.

C. Connection of the rapture to the Day of the Lord

1. Deliverance of the just immediately before delivery of judgment

Paul wrote each of his letters to the Thessalonians as a undivided whole; the division of the letter into chapters and verses was added later. In I

Thessalonians 4:13-17, Paul deals with what happens to believers, dead or alive, when Christ returns. This is the subject of the rapture, the time when believers are caught up in the air to be with the Lord. But when chapter 4 ends and chapter 5 begins, Paul is discussing a new subject, although the overall subject is still the end of the last days.

In chapter 5, verses 1-9 deal with the Day of the Lord, which is God's wrath upon unbelievers. While the Thessalonian believers *did not know* the series of events in 4:13-17 (the rapture), they *did know* full well about the Day of the Lord, 5:1-11. The point is that Paul moved directly from the subject of the rapture to the subject of God's wrath in the Day of the Lord.

Similarly, Paul ties the coming of the Lord and the "gathering together" (the rapture) together with the Day of the Lord in his *second* letter to the Thessalonians, both in chapter 1 and in chapter 2. Chapter 1, verses 6 through 10 set out the two-fold purpose of the Lord's coming: (1) to grant relief to those who are afflicted; and (2) to deal out retribution to unrepentant unbelievers in God's Day of the Lord wrath. In chapter 2, verses 1 through 3 also tie these two purposes together. Verse 1 states: "... with regard to the coming of our Lord Jesus Christ, and our gathering together to Him..." This verse speaks of the coming of the Lord Jesus Christ and the gathering together to Him in one breath, so to speak. The verse is describing an event, first from the heavenly point of view and then, second, from the earthly point of view. In other words, from the heavenly point of view, the Lord Jesus Christ comes out of heaven, and, from the earthly point of view, believers are gathered up into the skies to meet Him. That would accomplish the *first purpose* of His coming, which is to give relief to those who are afflicted. Then, with believers safely out of the way, He would begin to fulfill the *second purpose* of His coming, which is to deal out retribution to those who do not know God and who do not obey the gospel. This is a description of the Day of the Lord, which Paul now mentions in verse 2 of chapter 2.

Thus, these first three verses of II Thessalonians 2 clarify that the Lord Jesus Christ is coming not only to collect His own in the rapture, but also to punish the unbelievers in the Day of the Lord:

II Thessalonians 2
> [1]*Now we request you, brethren, with regard to the **coming of our Lord Jesus Christ**, and our **gathering together to Him**, [2]that you may not be quickly shaken from your composure or be disturbed either by a spirit or a message or a letter as if from us, to the effect that **the day of the Lord has come**. [3]Let no one in any way deceive you, for it will not come unless the apostasy comes first, and the man of lawlessness is revealed, the son of destruction...*

The two events of II Thessalonians 2:1 – the coming of the Lord and the gathering together to Him – are tied to the Day of the Lord in verse 2. Verse 3 appears to do the same. The "it" that will not come until the events listed thereafter may refer simply to the Day of the Lord, or it may refer to the Lord's coming for the dual purposes of gathering together His own and pouring out His wrath in the Day of the Lord.

If these two events (that is, the rapture and the Day of the Lord) were *not* tied together as dual purposes of His coming, then there would be no reason for the Thessalonian believers to "be quickly shaken from your composure or be disturbed either by a spirit or a message or a letter as if from us, to the effect that the day of the Lord has come." They understood that, when the Lord came again, He would rapture believers out of the world, and *then* the Day of the Lord would begin. If this false message that they had received to the effect that the Day of the Lord had already come were true, then that would mean that they had missed out on the rapture and were, in every sense of the words, "left behind." That is why they were distressed, and that is why Paul had to write this second letter to them. He wanted to reassure them that the Day of the Lord had not yet come. Since they understood that the rapture would immediately precede the Day of the Lord, he was telling them that they had not missed the rapture. Moreover, he gave them additional information: neither the rapture nor the Day of the Lord would happen *until* the "apostasy" had occurred and *until* the man of lawlessness, the son of destruction, was revealed. This revelation of the true identity of the antichrist will occur at the midpoint of the 70th week, as discussed in chapter 3 of this book, and again in subsection C. 1. (b) of this chapter 4.

This connection between the gathering together (the rapture) and the Day of the Lord is not limited to these two letters to the Thessalonians. Every description of the rapture takes place in the context of the signs in the heavens and on earth (the cataclysmic upheavals) of the onset of the Day of the Lord. This is the case in the three synoptic Gospels, in Matthew 24:29-31 and 37-44; in Mark 13:24-27; and in Luke 17:24-36. The final description of the rapture just prior to the onset of the Day of the Lord occurs in Revelation 6:12-7:1 and 7:9 to 8:1; then the trumpet judgments begin in Revelation 8:6. In every one of those passages, the rapture or deliverance comes first, and then judgment comes down immediately following.

In fact, not only in the context of the final rapture of the saints, but also in every passage regarding God's judgment, deliverance of the just is always tied directly to the delivery of judgment. According to Genesis 7:11, on the *same day* that Noah and his family entered the ark, "all the fountains of the great deep burst open, and the floodgates of the sky were opened."

In the case of Lot and his family's deliverance before the judgment of Sodom and Gomorrah, the angel told them to hurry in their escape, because he could not do anything until they arrived in Zoar. Genesis 19:23-24 records that:

> [23]*The sun had risen over the earth when Lot came to Zoar.* [24]*Then the Lord rained on Sodom and Gomorrah brimstone and fire from the Lord out of heaven...*

The minute that Lot and his family were safely out of the way, the Lord's judgment rained down from heaven.

Jesus Himself discussed these very same two judgments in the context of His teachings about His return at the end of times, the last of the last days; Matthew 24:37-44, are explicit comparisons:

MATTHEW 24

37For the coming of the Son of Man will be just like the days of Noah. 38For as in those days which were before the flood they were eating and drinking, they were marrying and giving in marriage, until the day that Noah entered the ark [this is a picture of the deliverance of the believer], *39and they* [the unbelievers] *did not understand until the flood came and took them all away;* **so shall the coming of the Son of Man be.** *40Then there shall be two men in the field; one will be taken, and one will be left. 41Two women will be grinding at the mill; one will be taken, and one will be left.* [Doesn't this sound like a description of the rapture? The one taken up would be a believer who is still alive and remaining at the time that the Lord returns, and the one left behind would be the unbeliever.] *42Therefore be on the alert, for you do not know which day your Lord is coming. 43But be sure of this, that if the head of the house had known at what time of the night the thief was coming, he would have been on the alert and would not have allowed his house to be broken into. 44For this reason you be ready too; for the Son of Man is coming at an hour when you do not think He will.*

In other words, Jesus is saying, because you have been taught and you now know that the Lord will return like a thief in the night, you – believers – be alert and ready at all times. If you are, then His return will be like a thief in the night only for the unbelievers because they are not expecting Him, as you are, or should be.

There is a parallel passage in Luke 17, beginning at verse 26.

Luke 17

²⁶And just as it happened in the days of Noah, so it shall be also in the days of the Son of Man: ²⁷they were eating, they were drinking, they were marrying, they were being given in marriage, **until the day** *that Noah entered the ark* [that is the deliverance, the rescue], *and the flood* [that is the judgment] *came and destroyed them all. ²⁸It was the same as happened in the days of Lot: they were eating, they were drinking, they were buying, they were selling, they were planting, they were building; ²⁹but* **on the day** [actually, the literal translation of the Greek is "on the same day"] *that Lot went out from Sodom* [that is the deliverance, the rescue] *it rained fire and brimstone from heaven and destroyed them all* [that is the judgment]. *³⁰***It will be just the same on the day that the Son of Man is revealed***... ³⁴I tell you, on that night there will be two men in one bed; one will be taken, and the other will be left. ³⁵There will be two women grinding at the same place; one will be taken, and the other will be left.*

These two parallel passages in the Gospels of Matthew and Luke are reinforced by Paul's teaching about the Day of the Lord in I Thessalonians 5. It seems that, at least for *unbelievers*, the days preceding the Day of the Lord judgment will seem like business as usual, because they will not have been suffering under the persecution of the antichrist. Thus, they will not be expecting judgment and it will come upon them suddenly and there will be no escape. Just as Jesus Himself tied together the deliverance of the rapture with the judgment of the Day of the Lord, Paul later did the same thing in I Thessalonians 4 and 5, and in II Thessalonians 2:1-3.

There is a picture of deliverance or rescue first. In the case of Noah, he and his family entered the ark. In the case of Sodom and Gomorrah, Lot and his family were escorted out of the city. In the future event, the rapture, believers will be taken and unbelievers will be left behind. Then, immediately after the deliverance, the Lord's judgment came. In the case of Noah, it was the flood that destroyed the whole earth. In the case of Sodom and Gomorrah, fire and brimstone rained down from heaven and destroyed the two cities. After the future event, the rapture, judgment will again follow immediately. Matthew 24:38-39 say that *just as it was in those days*, "so shall the coming of the Son of Man be."

As soon as Christ delivers or raptures believers out of the world, the wrath of God will be poured out on unbelievers in the time period known as the Day of the Lord. II Peter 3:7 describes the Day of the Lord as a day of judgment and destruction of ungodly men. Its purpose is punishment, a day of reckoning, vengeance, doom, wrath, and retribution upon all those who have refused to submit to the Lordship of a Savior.

Summary: When Jesus Christ comes again, the dead in Christ will be raised first. Their spirits will come with him when He comes, and He will somehow locate and reconstitute their bodies into imperishable resurrection bodies and reunite their bodies with their spirits. Any believers still alive when He comes will be caught up together with the formerly dead believers in the clouds to meet the Lord in the air, and thus all believers shall always be with the Lord.

This deliverance, this rescue, of the just will precede the delivery of God's judgment upon the unjust. Immediately after every last *believer* has been raptured from the earth, the wrath of God will be poured out in full measure on the unrepentant *unbelievers* in a period of time that is known as the Day of the Lord. It will come like a thief in the night as far as they are concerned, because they will not be expecting judgment at all, much less judgment at that time. It will be a terrible time when unbelievers will pay the penalty of eternal destruction, away from the presence of the Lord, and from the glory of His power. In contrast, *believers* will not be overtaken by the Day of the Lord, because, according to Romans 5:9 and I Thessalonians 1:10 and 5:9, they are not destined for wrath but for obtaining salvation through the Lord Jesus Christ.

2. Timing of both the rapture and the Day of the Lord

In II Thessalonians 1:6-8, Paul wrote to the persecuted church there that "it is only just for God to repay with affliction those who afflict you, and to give relief to you who are afflicted and to us as well when the Lord Jesus shall be revealed from heaven with His mighty angels in flaming fire, dealing out retribution to those who do not know God and to those who do not obey the gospel of our Lord Jesus." In these verses, Paul sets out very plainly the two purposes of the Lord's coming again. The first is "to give relief to you who are afflicted" and the second is "dealing out retribution to those who do not know God and to those who do not obey the gospel of our Lord Jesus."

In chapter 2, verses 1 through 3, of this same letter, Paul gives us a time clue. This promised relief from their affliction, which would happen at the coming of the Lord and the gathering together of His people to Himself – that's verse 1, *and* the Day of the Lord – that's verse 2 – would not come until Jesus was revealed from heaven with His mighty angels in flaming fire. *And* Jesus would not be revealed from heaven with His mighty angels in flaming fire *until* two other things occurred first. These two things are listed in verse 3. They are: (1) the apostasy; and (2) the revelation of the man of lawlessness, the son of destruction.

(a) After the apostasy

The English word, apostasy, is derived from the Greek *apostasia*, which means a defection from truth, a falling away from the faith. We are certainly seeing a rise in apostasy in America today. Some atheists are claiming that the constitutional freedom of religion means the freedom from religion. They want to eradicate all vestiges of the nation's Christian foundations. But there are other forms of apostasy, apart from people completely renouncing the Christian faith. Apostasy can and does exist within Christian churches and within entire Christian denominations, both in America and in other countries. This form of apostasy is based on the rejection of the Bible as the word of God, and consists of a cafeteria-style Christianity, in which the leaders pick and choose which parts of the Bible they like and want to keep, and they disregard the rest as irrelevant or just plain wrong. They have substituted man for God as the ultimate arbiter of truth, and they have reinvented God in their own image.

Despite the increased speed down the slippery slope of apostasy, it is unlikely that America's abandonment of God is the fulfillment of the particular apostasy prophesied in II Thessalonians 2:3. In the text of this verse, the word "apostasy" is used with the definite article: "the" apostasy. This is a reference to a future event that will parallel that particular time in Jewish history when the Israelites apostasized, or abandoned their faith, and sold out to Antiochus Epiphanes and his paganistic religion before and after he desecrated the Temple in 168 B.C. In this future apostasy, the Jews in Israel will enter into the covenant with the antichrist at the beginning of Daniel's 70th week, mistakenly believing that they are securing Israel's protection by doing so. This will amount to a wholesale abandonment of God in favor of the man whose identity as the man of lawlessness and the son of destruction will not be revealed until he commits the abomination of desolation spoken of by Daniel the prophet, in the middle of the 70th week. This is "the" apostasy.

The increasing apostasy of the Christian Church, especially in the Western world, will simply facilitate the rise of the antichrist into a position of power. In fact, the leaders of the world's mainline denominations may overtly support the antichrist; so the apostasy of the Western Christian Church may be a part of "the" apostasy by the Jews as these leaders support or perhaps even push for the Jews to enter into this covenant with the antichrist, the covenant that will begin the running of Daniel's 70th week.

Summary: "The" apostasy refers to the future time when Israel will enter into a covenant with the antichrist. Since II Thessalonians 2:1-3 places the coming of the Lord for the rapture and for the Day of the Lord *after* "the" apostasy, His coming cannot be before the beginning of the 70th week.

(b) After the Revelation of the Man of Lawlessness

The Greek word for "lawlessness" is *anomia*. This word means not the absence of law, but the rejection of the law, or will, of God, and the substitution of the will of self. It is the defiance of God's law. Verse 4 of chapter 2 of II Thessalonians explicitly specifies the blatant defiance of the antichrist, the man of lawlessness. He "opposes and exalts himself above every so-called god or object of worship, so that he takes his seat in the Temple of God, displaying himself as being God." Verse 9 of this same chapter 2 tells us that the coming of this man of lawlessness will be in accord with the activity of Satan. Clearly, this is an extraordinarily evil man. When he goes into the Temple of God – which can refer only to the to-be-rebuilt Jewish Temple in Jerusalem – and he sets up his throne, displaying himself as being God, it is logical to conclude that, if he is displaying himself as being God, he will demand that the world worship him as God. Revelation 13:12 confirms that all those who dwell on the earth will be compelled to worship the "first beast," who is the antichrist.

There is a close parallel to II Thessalonians 2:4 in Daniel 11:36, which says: "Then the king [a reference to the antichrist] will do as he pleases, and he will exalt and magnify himself above every god, and will speak monstrous things against the God of gods..." This act, this display of himself as being God as he takes his seat in the Temple of God, is probably the abomination of desolation referred to by Daniel the prophet. Since Daniel 9:27 indicates that the abomination of desolation will occur at the midpoint of the 70th week, that means that the revelation of the antichrist as the man of lawlessness will occur at the midpoint of the 70th week.

Summary: According to II Thessalonians 2:1-3, the coming of the Lord to rapture His own out of the world and to pour out His wrath in the Day of the Lord cannot occur until *after* the revelation of the antichrist as the man of lawlessness. That revelation of his true identity will occur at the midpoint of the 70th week. Therefore, the rapture cannot occur before the midpoint of the 70th week.

(c) After the Great Tribulation

Jesus taught, in Matthew 24:15-21 and following, that the abomination of desolation would trigger the onset of what He called the Great Tribulation. Verse 15 reads: "[W]hen you see the abomination of desolation which was spoken of through Daniel the prophet, standing in the holy place (let the reader understand)... [verse 21] *then* there will be a Great Tribulation, such as has not occurred since the beginning of the world until now, nor ever shall." Speaking of the same time period, Daniel 12:1 employs similar language: "Now at that time... there will be a time of distress such as never occurred since there was a nation until that time..."

Daniel 9:27, which describes the 70th week, discloses that, in the middle of this 70th week (which means 3½ years into the seven-year period), the antichrist will stop the Mosaic sacrificial system which will have been reinstituted, and will commit an abomination that so desolates the Temple from the top ("wing") down that it can no longer be considered a holy place.

Here is how Daniel describes it in chapter 9, verse 27: "And he [a reference to the antichrist] will make a firm covenant with the many [Israel] for one week [which means a period of seven years], but in the middle of the week [meaning 3½ years into this time period of seven years] he will put a stop to sacrifice and grain offering; and on the wing of abominations will come one who makes desolate, even until a complete destruction, one that is decreed, is poured out on the one who makes desolate."

The commission of the abomination of desolation, at the midpoint of the final seven-year period, triggers the Great Tribulation. The duration of the Great Tribulation is described variously in Daniel and in Revelation as "a time, times, and half a time," as "42 months," and as "1260 days," all of which mean 3½ years. Why will this be a time of "Great Tribulation?" The answer is: because the antichrist will be demanding that the entire world worship him as God. And Christians will refuse to do so. Revelation 13 describes the activity of the antichrist, beginning at verse 6:

Revelation 13
⁶And he [the antichrist] *opened his mouth in blasphemies against God, to blaspheme His name and His tabernacle, that is, those who dwell in heaven. ⁷And it was given to him to make war with the saints* [that means Christians] *and to overcome them; and authority over every tribe and people and tongue and nation was given to him. ⁸And all who dwell on the earth will worship him, everyone whose name has not been written from the foundation of the world in the book of life of the Lamb who has been slain.* [This means that **unbelievers** will obey the command of the antichrist to worship him as God.]

Verse 15 of this same passage in Revelation 13 declares explicitly that the antichrist will "cause as many as do not worship the image of the beast [that's the antichrist] to be killed." During this terrible time, the antichrist will hunt down and persecute and kill both Jews and Christians in a manner that will make the holocaust of World War II pale by comparison. With the explosion of technology at his command, the antichrist and his massive bureaucracy will be able to track down and register every human being on the planet. Jews and Christians will be hunted down and captured. Executions will be so common that *no believers* (referred to as "the elect" in Matthew 24:22) would survive if God did not cut short the days of the Great Tribulation.

Matthew 24:22 says: "And unless those days had been cut short, no life would have been saved; but for the sake of the elect those days shall be cut short." This does not mean that the Lord will cut short the 3½-year time period that is the latter half of the 70th week, but rather that the days of the Great Tribulation will not last the entire 3½ years.

The Lord continued His teaching, explaining what will happen when He cuts short the days of the Great Tribulation. Beginning at verse 29, Jesus explained:

Matthew 24

> [29] **But immediately after the tribulation of those days** the sun will be darkened, and the moon will not give its light, and the stars will fall from the sky, and the powers of the heavens will be shaken, [30] and then the sign of the Son of Man will appear in the sky, and then all the tribes of the earth will mourn, and they will see the Son of Man coming on the clouds of the sky with power and great glory. [31] And He will send forth His angels with a great trumpet and they **will gather together His elect** from the four winds, from one end of the sky to the other.

Summary: In Matthew 24:29-31, the Lord explicitly told His followers when He would return to rapture them out of the world. It will be not only *after* "the" apostasy, when the covenant between the antichrist and Israel is signed or strengthened; not only *after* the midpoint of the 70th week, when the identity of the man of lawlessness is revealed; but also *after* the Great Tribulation, which He will cut short so that the antichrist will not be able to accomplish his goal of annihilating every last Jew and Christian from the face of the earth.

All these passages from Daniel, from Matthew's Gospel, and from Paul's two epistles to the Thessalonians tie together, and together they provide a more complete picture of what Christians should expect if they are alive on the earth during those tumultuous last seven years, or for some portion of them. Setting out the sequence of events clarifies the timing of the return of the Lord to rapture His followers out of the world and to pour out His wrath in the Day of the Lord judgment:

When the antichrist enters into a covenant (or strengthens an existing covenant) with Israel, "the" apostasy begins. As the Jews trust their security to this man of lawlessness, unaware of his diabolical intentions, they will have abandoned the only true Source of safety and security and peace; they will have "apostasized." At the midpoint of Daniel's 70th week, the antichrist will go into the re-built Temple in Jerusalem, stop the re-instituted sacrifices and offerings, and he will commit the abomination of desolation as, according to II Thessalonians 2:4, he "opposes and exalts himself above every so-called god or object of worship, so that he takes his seat in the Temple of God, displaying himself as being God." With this blasphemous act, his true identity as the man of lawlessness will be revealed. And then the Great Tribulation will begin; this reign of terror of this Satan-inspired and perhaps Satan-possessed man will last for some period just shy of 3½ years. The Lord will, at some point before the end of the 70th week, cut short the days of the Great Tribulation, and erupt out of heaven with a shout, with the voice of the archangel, and with the trumpet of God. He will send forth His angels with a great trumpet and they will gather together His elect – first the dead believers, then the living – from the four winds, from one end of the sky to the other. Then the Day of the Lord judgment will begin. At the onset of the Day of the Lord, the Lord will render the lawless one inoperative by His appearance, and the Lord will at some point thereafter, before the time period that is known as the Day of the Lord ends, slay the man of lawlessness with the breath of His mouth. Also, in the Day of the Lord, unbelievers will pay the penalty of eternal destruction, away from the presence of the Lord and from the glory of His power.

• 5 •

How do Christians prepare for the Great Tribulation?

A. Submission to the Lordship of Jesus Christ

Given the explosion in technological advances in recent decades, and its continuing exponential expansion into every aspect of our daily lives, those with eyes to see cannot help but imagine that the time is rapidly drawing close in which the "science fiction" of Revelation 13 becomes reality. Computer chips that exist as I write in late 2013 may be obsolete in a matter of months, replaced by a much higher grade and yet smaller device. The rapidity of change and the virtual evaporation of personal privacy have generated an intense sense of urgency on my part, to sound the alarm, to send out the warning to people who call themselves Christians, to use whatever time we may have left to prepare spiritually for eternity. How does one do that?

The first step is to examine yourself. Are you really a Christian? If you were to die today, and stand before the throne of God Almighty, what answer would you give to the question why He should allow you to spend eternity in heaven with Him? Here are some of the usual answers:

- I am basically a good person; I have done more good things than bad things.
- I have given money to the church.
- I have attended church regularly (or at least most Christmases and Easters).

- I have donated time and money to charitable causes.
- My parents and all my family were/are Christians.
- I have done the best I could with the hand I was dealt in this life.
- I have endured abuse at the hands of (fill in the blank).

All these responses are based on the assumptions that one can either *earn* the right to enter heaven, or *be* good enough to enter. Both are Biblically unfounded and dangerously wrong. A quick review of the Old Testament concept of redemption will explain why.

1. Why people need a Savior, a Redeemer

The Biblical concept of *kinsman redeemer* has its roots in the Old Testament practice in which an Israelite who could not pay his debts would then either sell his land or sell himself or his family into slavery to pay the debt. When that happened, the Law set out, in Leviticus chapter 25, the procedure for "redeeming" or buying back the land or the person. A redeemer had to be a blood relative who had the ability to pay the ransom to buy back his relative or his relative's land, because the redeemed relative was helpless and without the means to pay. The kinsman, the relative, had a duty, an obligation, to redeem the enslaved relative or the land that had been sold if he could. If he could not or if he refused to fulfill his obligation, then the right and responsibility passed to the next qualified man. If you have studied the book of Ruth, you know that that is how Boaz was able to marry Ruth.

In the case of mankind as a whole, why was redemption necessary? The answer is in the first book of the Bible, Genesis. In chapter 2, God created Adam, the first man, and entrusted him with stewardship over the world. In verses 16 and 17, God told Adam that he could eat freely from any tree in the garden – except from the tree of the knowledge of good and evil. And, because He wanted Adam to love Him out of his own free will, God gave Adam the freedom to choose whether or not to love Him back. Adam could show God that he was returning God's love by obeying the one command God had given him: not to eat from the tree of the knowledge of good and evil.

But Genesis 3 records the exchange between Satan (who is described in Revelation 12 as the great dragon, the serpent of old, the devil, and Satan) and Eve, in which Satan convinced Eve that God did not really have her best interest at heart and that God did not want her to be like Him. Because she was deceived, she disobeyed the one command of God; and Adam, although he was not deceived, also disobeyed. This is known as the fall of man.

In disobeying the one command of God, Adam abdicated his dominion over the world which God had created for his enjoyment. Satan usurped that role, and has been the ruler over this world ever since that time. *See* John 12:31; 14:30; 16:11; and Ephesians 2:2 (there he is called the prince of the power of the air). All of mankind, born *of Adam*, has been born into slavery to Satan, and all of creation was also subjected to the curse of Adam's fall. Because all men were born into slavery, it is our nature to sin, and we are in bondage, chained to Satan by our sins. We were born into his kingdom and if nothing changes before we die, we will not go to heaven when we die. We are helpless to earn or to purchase our own release from slavery to Satan. There is not one thing, or a lifetime of things, we can *do* that will merit our entrance into heaven. Nor will we ever *be* good enough. Therefore, all of mankind – and creation – need a kinsman redeemer to come and buy us back out of slavery. The price of our redemption was set out by God as the blood of a perfect human being. Hebrews 9:22 says: "Without the shedding of blood, there is no forgiveness of sins." Since no human being born in Adam is perfect (because we are all born in slavery to Satan and to sin), God provided our Kinsman Redeemer by incarnating His Son. Jesus would be a *blood relative* of mankind, made flesh and blood, but *not* a son of Adam, because He was born of the seed of God. He lived a perfect life, keeping the Law perfectly, and therefore qualified in His perfection to act as our Redeemer. Philippians 2 says that He was obedient to the point of death, even death on a cross. When He shed His blood for our redemption,

God the Father accepted His act of sacrifice as sufficient payment for the redemption of mankind and creation, to purchase them back from slavery to sin and Satan. Although the price of redemption was paid in full at the cross, however, the practical application of that judgment has not yet occurred.

2. The double transfer

But even having our sins paid for by a perfectly sinless Kinsman Redeemer is *still* not enough to get us into heaven. Although the price of our redemption was paid in full, we ourselves have to be righteous, perfect. That means we have to conform to all the demands of God's law. This sounds like going back to rules, doesn't it? You must do this, you mustn't do that. But it's not. What has happened is that God the Son has not only taken all your sins onto Himself and paid the penalty for them Himself, but He has also transferred back to you His perfect ability to do what is right in God's eyes. It's a double exchange: you give your sins to Jesus, so He can pay the penalty for them; then He gives you His righteousness, so that you can please God. This double exchange is described in II Corinthians 5:21, which says that God the Father made God the Son, who was perfect and never committed one sin, to become sin on our behalf, so that we might become the righteousness of God in Him.

Satan did not and does not want even one human soul to be redeemed from slavery to him by this great Kinsman Redeemer. Thus, the sweeping panorama of human history recorded in the Bible from Genesis to Revelation has reflected the spiritual battle raging across God's creation, as Satan has attempted, time and again, to thwart, first the birth of this Redeemer, and then to destroy Him, and to destroy those of His kingdom. If Satan were able to destroy all the subjects of Christ's kingdom, then perhaps there would be no Second Coming, because there would be nothing to come to reclaim. The entirety of Revelation 12 gives us an overview of this ongoing struggle. Verse 7 tells us: "And there was war in heaven, Michael and his angels waging war with the dragon [Satan]. And the dragon and *his* angels waged war." We don't usually think of heaven as a place where war is waged, but this battle is on a cosmic scale. While the Bible reveals the end of the story, making it plain that Satan will lose this war in the end, the question for each individual is: to whom do you belong? Are you still under the dominion of Satan, a slave to sin, or have you claimed the pardon that was purchased at so great a cost; have you entered into the kingdom of Christ?

As much as each individual would like to be the master of his fate and the captain of his soul (William Ernest Henley, 1849-1903, *Invictus*), the truth is that we are all subject to one king or the other King. If you are in slavery to Satan, then you will obey him, because, as a slave, you have no choice. On the other hand, being the subject of the King means that you learn all you can about what pleases your sovereign Lord, and you obey His commands. Romans 5:8, says this: "But God demonstrates His own love toward us, in that while we were yet sinners, Christ died for us." Would not any reasonable person choose to serve a Lord who would love him so much that He would lay down His life for him?

Summary: From the time of Adam's fall, all men are born in slavery to Satan, sin, and death. God the Son took on flesh and became the Relative, the Kinsman, of sinful man. Fully God and fully man, but not born of Adam, He lived a perfect life and qualified to pay the price to redeem, to buy back, man from his bondage in slavery. Those who choose to acknowledge His finished work on the cross on their behalf and who choose to avail themselves of the pardon He purchased at an unfathomable cost, have their sins transferred to Him, and His righteousness transferred back to them. Thereafter, they are subjects of the King of Kings. When they die, and stand before the throne of God Almighty, and they are asked why He should allow them to spend eternity in heaven with Him, the answer they will give is that they have been purchased with the blood of the Redeemer; He has paid in full for their sins, and His righteousness has been transferred to them. They know whose they are; they are His!

B. Growing relationship with Jesus Christ

Understanding that you need a Redeemer to save you from eternal separation from God and all that is good is only the beginning. So is the next necessary step, which is to make an affirmative decision to enter into a relationship with Jesus Christ, God the Son, and, through Him, with God the Father. You acknowledge to Him that you have sinned and are not worthy to go to heaven and to be in the presence of God. You thank Him for paying the penalty for your sins for you. That is how you give your sins over to Him. Now for the other part of the exchange: you accept the pardon that you may receive as a result of His death on the cross. *AND* you actively submit your life to His authority. That means you start with words – saying you are submitting your life to Him – and then you start building a relationship with Him. You may or may not experience His love as a feeling, but what really matters is not your feelings, but your commitment.

How do you build a relationship with the almighty, eternal, omnipotent, omniscient God? Consider the relationships you have with other people. How do you know about them – what they like, don't like, how they talk, expressions they use, whether they are trustworthy or not? The answer is, by spending time with them and interacting with them.

The same principle applies in a relationship with God. But since God is a Spirit (John 4:24), how can we know Him? Through His Son, Jesus. But Jesus, the man, died 2,000 years ago; so how can we know *Him*? The answer is: through the words He left behind, which we know as the Bible. In fact, John 1:1 calls Jesus "the Word." He is God the Father's Word to us. God is revealed in Jesus. So if we want to know Him, and be in a relationship with Him, we have to spend time with Him – and the way we do that is by spending time reading His written Word, and thinking about what it says. It takes time, and it takes discipline to set aside the time. But we manage to find time to eat several times a day, to maintain our physical bodies. We should give at least as much attention to our spiritual nourishment. Just as you would not expect a baby to grow and thrive if you did not feed him, you can hardly expect a different principle to operate for spiritual babies, children, or even mature Christians. Because our spirits will live on in eternity, consider the time spent in this life building your relationship with Jesus Christ as an eternal investment, one you cannot lose.

I cannot over-emphasize the point that Christianity is all about relationship, not religion. It's not about duty and rules; it's about actions you take because you love Someone and want to please Him. It is not enough to say one prayer, accepting Jesus Christ "as your Lord and Savior," and then to return to your life as it was before. Too many people today are happy to have Jesus as a Savior, but they don't want Him to be their Lord! Submission to the Lordship of Jesus Christ begins with an understanding of what is meant by the similar statements in Acts 16:31 and Romans 10:9:

Believe in the Lord Jesus, and you shall be saved... (Acts 16:31)

...if you confess with your mouth Jesus as Lord, and believe in your heart that God raised Him from the dead, you shall be saved. (Romans 10:9)

"Believing" is much more than believing that Jesus Christ exists and that He is God the Son. After all, even demons believe that, and then they shudder, according to James 2:19. They acknowledged Him as the Son of God and submitted to His authority in Matthew 8:29, Mark 1:34, Mark 5:5, Luke 4:41, and Luke 8:28. But it is safe to say that they are not going to heaven, ever. Clearly, something more than an intellectual understanding of who He is, is involved in "believing."

A commonplace example may serve to demonstrate the kind of belief that is required for salvation:

A husband calls his stay-at-home wife from his office and tells her that he is on his way home, and asks her to start cooking dinner so that they can get to an evening engagement on time. She says, "All right," and hangs up the phone. Then, instead of going into the kitchen, she returns to what she was doing before her husband called. Even if she really believed he was coming home, her inaction in response means that this is, at best, mere intellectual assent. This is not the kind of belief that the Bible requires for salvation.

Now take the same example, but this time, when the wife hangs up the phone, she goes into the kitchen and starts preparing the dinner. *This* is much more than intellectual assent, because she acted on her belief that her husband was really coming home. Moreover, her action was to comply with his request, and, one may assume that, from the fact that they married one another, her compliance was founded on her love for him.

Jesus made it plain while He walked and taught on this earth that a relationship of love and obedience was the key to salvation; in Matthew 7, He warned:

> [21]*Not everyone who says to Me, "Lord, Lord," will enter the kingdom of heaven; but he who does the will of My Father who is in heaven.* [22]*Many will say to Me on that day, "Lord, Lord, did we not prophesy in Your name, and in Your name cast out demons, and in Your name perform many miracles?"* [23]*And then I will declare to them, "I never knew you; depart from Me, you who practice lawlessness."*

Notice that these were people who prophesied in His name! And cast out demons and performed miracles in His name! They were the equivalent of today's "name-droppers," people who think they gain status by claiming to know some famous personage; the problem is that the famous person doesn't know them, because they have never spent time in each other's company. It is the same with Jesus. If you don't want to know Him while you are here in this life, why would you want to know Him in the next? Why would you want to spend eternity with Him? More importantly, if you never wanted to spend time in His company during this life, why would *He* want to spend time in *your* company in the next?

Notice also that Jesus characterized the one who *will* enter the kingdom of heaven as the one "who does the will of My Father who is in heaven."

Only the person who has spent time reading and studying and thinking about the Bible, and spent time praying and listening for His voice, can *know* what the will of God is so that he can do it. Obedience is not possible if one doesn't know what is meant to be obeyed. Jesus reinforced His point with an illustration in the next few verses of Matthew 7:

> *²⁴Therefore everyone who hears these words of Mine, and **acts upon them**, may be compared to a wise man, who built his house upon the rock. ²⁵And the rain descended, and the floods came, and the winds blew, and burst against that house; and yet it did not fall, for it had been founded upon the rock. ²⁶And everyone who hears these words of Mine, and **does not act upon them**, will be like a foolish man, who built his house upon the sand. ²⁷And the rain descended, and the floods came, and the winds blew, and burst against that house; and it fell, and great was its fall.*

The time you invest in studying the Bible will cause you to mature, to grow up spiritually. The reality is that, when you participate in the double exchange, God gives you much more than "His righteousness." What He gives you is Himself. In a way that we cannot fully understand, God the Holy Spirit comes to live in your heart and mind. You will spend the rest of your life learning to recognize His voice and learning to follow His lead. Just as you can never know another person completely, you will never know the Bible so well that you know God completely – not that that will *ever* be possible! This will be the most rewarding relationship of your life, for the rest of your life, and the rest of eternity. In fact, Jesus defined eternal life as a relationship with Himself and with God the Father. John 17:3 quotes Jesus saying: "[T]his is eternal life, that they may know Thee, the only true God, and Jesus Christ whom Thou hast sent."

Summary: Just as physical growth is the sign of life in human children, growing spiritual maturity founded on an ongoing, growing relationship with Jesus Christ is the sign of spiritual life. If we want Jesus to say He knows us, we will invest time and effort in our relationship with the Lord of not only the entire created order, but also of every detail of our lives.

C. Avoiding deception

The reason spiritual maturity will be critical during the time of the Great Tribulation is that familiarity with the Bible will be the best, indeed the only, defense against being deceived by the antichrist and his false prophet. The hallmark of the antichrist's operations will be deception. Of course, the problem with deception is that the one being deceived doesn't know that he is being deceived.

The best way for Satan to deceive people is *by using the Bible*. He's had several thousand years to learn the Old Testament, and, on top of that, he's had another 2,000 years to learn the New Testament. He knows it better than we do, and he will know how to use the Bible, the very Words of God, to deceive human beings. He will take a nugget of truth, and wrap it so convincingly in a lie that, unless we are truly practiced in discernment, we will be deceived. And it is entirely possible that, for those people who live in the time of the Great Tribulation, all Bibles will be confiscated. All that Christians will have to guide them will be what they have retained in their memories. Maybe that is why the psalmist wrote in Psalms 119:11: "I have stored up your word in my heart, that I might not sin against you." That's the ESV translation; other translations say, "I have hidden your word in my heart," or "I have treasured your word in my heart."

Deception was a critical subject that Paul addressed in his second letter to the Thessalonians. In fact, the letter itself was occasioned by a fake letter, ostensibly from him, that contained false teaching about the timing of the Day of the Lord, a letter that so deceived the Thessalonian believers that they were most distressed. In II Thessalonians 2:9 and 10, Paul wrote that the antichrist's "coming is in accord with the activity of Satan, with all power and signs and false wonders, and with all the *deception of wickedness* for those who perish, because they did not receive the love of the truth so as to be saved."

The Great Tribulation will be the most dangerous era in history for Christians. They will have to discern whether or not the world leader is indeed the antichrist, and if he is, they will have to refuse to take his mark and refuse to worship him. That means they must be prepared to die for their faith, because Revelation 13:15 says that all who refuse to worship the antichrist will be killed. Until the time that they are rounded up and forced to choose between taking the mark of the beast or being killed, Christians will not be able to buy or sell, so it is foreseeable that they will suffer from famine in the meantime.

The Lord's description of the Great Tribulation is in Matthew 24:9-26. Jesus warned His followers that they will suffer greatly and be killed, and be hated by all the nations because of His name. People will turn on each other and betray them. This time is called the *Great Tribulation* for a reason: so many believers will be killed that the Lord will have to cut the days of the Great Tribulation short.

The level of deception during this dangerous time in history will run so deep and be so difficult to pierce that many learned and knowledgeable people, including some leaders in the Church, will be deceived. Indeed, Jesus warned believers in Matthew 24:24 that the power and signs and false wonders of the false Christ and false prophet would be so great that they would deceive even the elect – if that were possible. Fortunately, the Greek phrase that is translated into English as, "if that were possible," makes it clear that true believers will not be deceived because they will be kept by the power of God. It will be only by the grace of God that the elect will stand firm.

How can we guard against deception? The answer is: by studying and knowing the Word of truth while it is still available to us. For example, Revelation 13:13 and 14 tell us *in advance* that the false prophet will be able to do the same thing that the prophet Elijah did, that is, call fire down from the sky:

Revelation 13

*[13]He performs great signs, so that he even makes fire come down out of heaven to the earth in the presence of men. [14]And **he deceives** those who dwell on the earth because of the signs which it was given him to perform in the presence of the beast* [that's the antichrist]...

Returning to Matthew 24, in the context of His teaching on His return after the Great Tribulation, Jesus again warned against the dangers of deception; in Matthew 24:23-27, He said:

[23]Then if anyone says to you, "Behold, here is the Christ," or "There He is," do not believe him. [24]For false Christs and false prophets will arise and will show great signs and wonders, so as to mislead [some translations say "deceive"], *if possible, even the elect. [25]Behold, I have told you in advance. [26]If therefore they say to you, "Behold, He is in the wilderness," do not go forth, or, "Behold, He is in the inner rooms," do not believe them. [27]For just as the lightning comes from the east, and flashes even to the west, so shall the coming of the Son of Man be.*

The Bible plainly teaches that no one will be able to miss the Second Coming of God the Son, because He will be coming directly out of heaven, riding on the clouds, and every eye will see Him. So don't be deceived by anyone telling you that Jesus Christ has come and is hiding in the wilderness, or for that matter, anywhere ON the planet. Continuing in Matthew 24:29ff, Jesus taught:

*[29]But immediately after the tribulation of those days the sun will be darkened, and the moon will not give its light, and the stars will fall from the sky, and the powers of the heavens will be shaken, [30]and then the sign of the Son of Man will appear in the sky, and then all the tribes of the earth will mourn, and **they will see the Son of Man coming on the clouds of the sky with power and great glory**. [31]And*

> *He will send forth His angels with a great trumpet and they will gather together His elect from the four winds, from one end of the sky to the other.*

Paul reinforced the Lord's teaching in his first letter to the Thessalonians:

I Thessalonians 4
> ¹⁶For **the Lord Himself will descend from heaven** *with a shout, with the voice of the archangel, and with the trumpet of God; and the dead in Christ shall rise first.* ¹⁷*Then we who are alive and remain shall be caught up together with them* **in the clouds to meet the Lord in the air**, *and thus we shall always be with the Lord.*

John reiterated this same teaching in Revelation 1:7: "Behold, He is coming *with the clouds,* and *every eye will see Him,* even those who pierced Him."

Indeed, the manner of Christ's return was not only foretold by Jesus Himself, but was confirmed by angels at the time of His ascension:

Acts 1
> ⁹*And after He had said these things, He was lifted up while they were looking on, and a cloud received Him out of their sight.* ¹⁰*And as they were gazing intently into the sky while He was departing, behold, two men in white clothing stood beside them;* ¹¹*and they also said, "Men of Galilee, why do you stand looking into the sky? This Jesus, who has been taken up from you into heaven,* **will come in just the same way as you have watched Him go into heaven.**"

Since deception will be integral to the antichrist's rise to power, Jesus repeatedly instructed His disciples, including us, to be aware, to be informed, and to be knowledgeable about the truth of His teaching:

See to it that no one misleads you. (Matthew 24:2)

See that you are not frightened. (Matthew 24:6)

Behold, I have told you in advance. (Matthew 24:25)

Therefore, be on the alert, for you do not know which day your Lord is coming. (Matthew 24:42)

You be ready, too. (Matthew 24:44)

Be on the alert then. (Matthew 25:13)

It is the individual believer's responsibility *not to be deceived.* Ephesians 4:14 reminds us: "[W]e are no longer to be children, tossed here and there by waves, and carried about by every wind of doctrine, by the trickery of men, by craftiness in deceitful scheming." There is that word again: "deceitful." We do not have the luxury of remaining as spiritual babies, who are gullible, and believe whatever they are told. The writer to the Hebrews said in chapter 5, verse 14: "But solid food is for the mature, who *because of practice* have their *senses trained to discern good and evil.*"

When God says He is going to do something, we can know for certain that it will come to pass. II Peter 1:19 says: "And so we have the prophetic word made more sure, to which you do well to *pay attention* as to a lamp shining in a dark place." In John 16:1, Jesus said: "These things I have spoken to you, that you may be kept from stumbling."

We may stumble and occasionally fall, but the Lord will pick us up because He has promised, in Philippians 1:6, that He has begun a good work in us and He will complete it until the day of Jesus Christ. Moreover, the Lord God has given us His Word so that we will know what is going to come to pass because He has told us beforehand. Amos 3:7 says: "Surely the Lord God does nothing unless He reveals His secret counsel to His servants the prophets." Through His prophet Isaiah (chapter 46), the Lord declared:

> *⁹...I am God, and there is no other; I am God, and there is no one like Me, ¹⁰declaring the end from the beginning and from ancient times things which have not been done, saying, "My purpose will be established, and I will accomplish all My good pleasure."*

He has told us the end from the beginning and that end will be good for those who are in Christ. The end, according to Daniel 2:44, is that God sets up the kingdom which will never be destroyed, and that kingdom will not be left for another people; it will crush and put an end to all those other kingdoms, but it will itself endure forever. Daniel 7:27 tells us that the sovereignty, the dominion, and the greatness of all the kingdoms under the whole heaven will be given to the people of the saints of the Highest One; His kingdom will be an everlasting kingdom, and all the dominions will serve and obey Him.

Summary: NOW, while we still have access to our Bibles, and the freedom to meet and to study the Bible together, is the time to be hiding His word in your heart. Read, pray, try to memorize. Feasting on the word of God is the only area of life in which moderation has no place. Build your relationship with Christ, and read your Bible every day!

D. Remaining faithful in "the strength of His might"

Although *unbelievers* will have no problem taking the mark of the beast and worshiping his image, every Christian who is alive during the Great Tribulation will be required to choose whether to submit to the mark of the beast and worship his image OR be killed. Those who refuse to take the mark and to worship the image of the beast will have chosen death, but that death will end their suffering forever and will be a glorious entrance into the presence of Jesus Christ in heaven. Conversely, those who submit to the mark of the beast and worship his image will not die immediately but will have chosen hades, and ultimately hell, the lake of fire. Purely from a logical point of view, having nothing to do with one's faith, a choice to worship the antichrist, take his mark, and "live" is a poor choice. These people will not live out their lives, having children, and grandchildren, and living productive, successful lives by the world's standards. In at most 3½ years, they will face the undiluted wrath of God, and will die horrible deaths, only to begin the real suffering as they "pay the penalty of eternal destruction, away from the presence of the Lord and from the glory of His power," according to II Thessalonians 1:9.

How are we to stand firm in our faith during the Great Tribulation? The answer is: not in our own strength. The flesh will fail us every time. But the grace of God is like manna; it is provided when it is needed. You cannot save it up, like a savings account, and you cannot hoard it. But, just at the precise moment that you need it, all you have to do is ask for it, and God's grace will rain down from heaven in abundance. Do not entertain for even one moment a doubt that He will not do whatever is necessary to sustain your faith. Romans 8:32 asks rhetorically: "He who did not spare His own Son, but delivered Him up for us all, how will He not also with Him freely give us all things?" In other words, if God the Father would pour out His unmitigated wrath on God the Son in order to purchase our redemption, don't you know that, having gone that far, He will do whatever is required to keep and to preserve those He purchased with His own lifeblood?

How will we stand firm? In the strength of HIS might. In Paul's prayer of Ephesians 1:18, he asks God to enlighten the eyes of our hearts, so that we may *know* for a certainty, among other things, "the surpassing greatness of His power toward us who believe." This surpassingly great power is "in accordance with the working of the **strength of His might** which He brought about in Christ, when He raised Him from the dead…" This is the power to resurrect the dead to life, in an imperishable body, not subject to the curse of decay, to live forever! *That* is the power that we can know and can call upon in our hour of need. *That* is the power that will infuse us with the strength to endure the unendurable, to bear the unbearable, all the while remaining faithful to His calling. First century Christians sang hymns of praise as they were fed to the lions or burned alive; it was that same power, "the strength of *His might*," given to them that is available to each Christian for the asking. Indeed, Paul exhorts every believer of every generation throughout the centuries to call upon this power. In the same letter to the Ephesians, in 6:10-11, Paul writes: "Finally, be strong in the Lord, and **in the strength of His might**. Put on the full armor of God, that you may be able to stand firm against the schemes of the devil."

Once more, how will we stand firm? In the strength of HIS might. According to Ephesians 3:20, it is He, and He alone, who "is able to do *exceeding abundantly beyond all that we ask or think, according to the power that works within us…*" This resurrection power of God, that is "exceeding abundant" beyond our imaginations, is the "power that works *within us!*" May we stand firm and faithful to our Lord, *in the strength of His might*, until He returns or calls us home.

Jude:

²⁴Now to Him who is able to keep you from stumbling, and to make you stand in the presence of His glory blameless with great joy, ²⁵to the only God our Savior, through Jesus Christ our Lord, be glory, majesty, dominion and authority, before all time and now and forever. Amen.

Afterword

A final note to my daughters, my husband, my sisters, my extended family, and to any reader of this book: I am fully aware that this book is not an easy one to read, not only because of the complexity of the material covered, but also because it is nothing short of terrifying. We think of the first century Christians eaten alive by lions in the Roman arenas, or of the atrocities of the holocaust of World War II, and we think that such heinous acts of cruelty could not possibly happen again. As a result, it is natural to be utterly repulsed by Jesus' characterization of the last 3½ years of the 70th week as a "great tribulation, such as has not occurred since the beginning of the world until now, nor ever shall" (Matthew 24:21). How can any tribulation be not only worse than the holocaust, but literally *unprecedented* in its horror? How can such a time of terror go on to the extent that almost no Christians survive to the time of the Lord's return? It is unthinkable. We cannot conceive of it. We don't want to try.

But it is this natural aversion to face these truths— truths which the Lord Himself taught— that puts Christians in real danger. The saying "forewarned is forearmed" applies here. We cannot afford to be ignorant of the coming storm, particularly when the hallmark of the antichrist's operations will be deception. The level of deception will be so great that Jesus warned that, if it were possible, even the elect would be deceived (Matthew 24:24). We cannot afford the luxury of closing our eyes to the realities of the times we live in, and to the real possibility— actually, probability— that we are fast approaching the time when all that was prophesied will begin to take place.

Our only defense against this onslaught of dark deception, of lies cloaked in Biblical language, will be to repent of our attachment to the ways of the world, and to turn back to the Lord in humility and in true fear. Let us get back into reading and studying the Bible, and nailing down our understanding of key verses and passages, even memorizing if possible. The day will come, sooner than we think, when all Bibles will be confiscated, and Christian gatherings for worship and study will be forbidden. Those to whom the average Christian would turn in such times will be taken away first: pastors, priests, Bible study teachers, authors of Christian books. We will be incarcerated and probably executed near the beginning of the Great Tribulation, as an example to frighten other Christians into submitting to the antichrist. That means we will not be here to counsel, comfort, teach, and guide other Christians who are caught unprepared to deal with the terror tactics of the antichrist. So my prayer for you and my plea to you is to use this book as a study manual that supplements your primary study of the Bible. Do not be among the many who will fall away from Jesus Christ when they are tested. Remember what Simon Peter said in response to Jesus' question whether he wanted to go away from Him: "Lord, to whom shall we go? You have the words of eternal life" (John 6:68). Then Peter added: "And we have believed and have come to know that You are the Holy One of God" (John 6:69).

My prayer for you, my beloved first-born, and my pearl of great price, and for so many others (including myself), is that we will endure, stand firm in the strength of His might, and rejoice eternally together in the presence of the Holy One of God.

Appendix

Biblical Descriptions of the Antichrist

from Daniel 2, 7, 9, 11
II Thessalonians 2
Revelation 11, 12, 13, 17

He is called the prince who is to come. He will descend from the people who destroyed Jerusalem and the Temple. (Daniel 9:26)

The beast comes up out of the abyss. (Revelation 11:7; 17:8)

He will make a firm covenant with "the many" for one week. (Daniel 9:27)

"The" apostasy, abandonment of the faith (the Jews' abandonment of God, evidenced by the signing of the covenant with the antichrist) begins. (II Thessalonians 2:3, Daniel 9:27)

The beast comes up out of the sea having 10 horns and seven heads and on his horns are 10 diadems, and on his head are blasphemous names. (Revelation 13:1)

The beast is described as scarlet, and full of blasphemous names, having seven heads and 10 horns, but no diadems. (Revelation 17:3)

While the seven heads represent seven PAST kings and kingdoms, the beast is himself an eighth, and he is one of the seven. (Revelation 17:11)

The 10 horns represent 10 FUTURE kings who give their power and authority to the beast. (Revelation 17:13)

Out of the fourth beast kingdom, 10 kings will arise; they are represented by the 10 horns. (Daniel 7:24)

A little horn comes up among the 10 horns and three of the first 10 horns are pulled out by the roots before it. The little horn has the eyes of a man. (Daniel 7:8,20,24)

The little horn is larger in appearance than its associates. (Daniel 7:20)

The little horn will be different from the previous ones (the 10 kings), and will subdue three kings. (Daniel 7:24)

The first beast who comes out of the sea is like a leopard, with feet like those of a bear, and a mouth like the mouth of a lion. (Revelation 13:2)

The coming of the man of lawlessness is in accord with the activity of Satan, with all power and signs and false wonders, and with all the deception of wickedness for those who perish, because they did not receive the love of the truth so as to be saved. (II Thessalonians 2:11)

The dragon, who represents Satan, gave the beast, who represents the antichrist, his power, his throne, and great authority. (Revelation 13:2)

He will do as he pleases. . . and he will prosper until the indignation is finished. (Daniel 11:36)

One of the heads of the beast was slain, but the fatal wound was healed. (Revelation 13:3,12,14)

The beast is described as one who "was, and is not, and is about to come up out of the abyss." (Revelation 17:8,11)

The beast is formidable, because the world wonders who is able to wage war with him. (Revelation 13:4)

He will honor with gold and treasures a foreign god of fortresses, a god whom his fathers did not know. (Daniel 11:38)

With the help of this foreign god, he will take action against the strongest of fortresses. (Daniel 11:39)

He will war against the king of the South and the king of the North, and he will enter countries, overflow them, and pass through. (Daniel 11:40)

He will also enter Israel, called the Beautiful Land. (Daniel 11:41)

Many countries, including Egypt, and Libya, and Ethiopia, will fall into his hand, but Edom, Moab, and the foremost of the sons of Ammon will be rescued out of his hand. (Daniel 11:41-43)

Rumors from the East and from the North will disturb him, and he will go forth with great wrath to destroy and annihilate many. (Daniel 11:44)

In the middle of the 70th week, he will put a stop to sacrifice and grain offering, and he will commit the abomination of desolation. (Daniel 9:27)

His identity as the man of lawlessness, the son of destruction, is revealed at this point – the middle of the 70th week – because he opposes and exalts himself above every so-called god or object of worship, so that he takes his seat in the Temple of God, displaying himself as being God. (II Thessalonians 2: 3b-4,8)

He will pitch the tents of his royal pavilion between the seas and the beautiful Holy Mountain. (Daniel 11:45)

He has a mouth speaking arrogant words and blasphemies against God, against His name, and against His tabernacle. (Revelation 13:5,6, Daniel 7:25)

The little horn utters great boasts. (Daniel 7:8,11,20)

He will exalt and magnify himself above every god, and will speak monstrous things against the God of gods. (Daniel 11:36)

He will show no regard for the gods of his fathers or for the desire of women, nor will he show regard for any other God; for he will magnify himself above them all. (Daniel 11:37)

He will be given authority to act for 42 months. (Revelation 13:5)

It will be given to him to make war with the saints and to overcome them; authority over every tribe and people and tongue and nation will be given to him. (Revelation 13:7, Daniel 7:21, 25 – this verse 25 adds that the saints will be given into his hand for a time, times, and half a time)

He will intend to make alterations in time and in law. (Daniel 7:26)

He will receive the worship of all who dwell on the earth – that is, unbelievers. (Revelation 13:8,12)

He will have a partner, called the second beast in Revelation 13:11, and the false prophet in Revelation 16:13, 19:20 and 20:10. This false prophet comes up out of the earth and has two horns like a lamb, but speaks as a dragon. (Revelation 13:11)

The false prophet exercises all his (the first beast's) authority in his presence. He performs great signs, including making fire come down out of heaven to the earth. (Revelation 13:12-13)

The false prophet deceives all those who dwell on the earth, and he requires them to make an image to the beast who was wounded but came to life. (Revelation 13:14)

The false prophet gives breath to this image, so that the image can speak and cause those who do not worship it to be killed. (Revelation 13:15)

The false prophet causes everyone to be given a mark on the right hand or on their forehead, which allows them to buy or to sell. (Revelation 13:16-17)

The beast will overcome the two witnesses and kill them. (Revelation 11:7)

The beast and the kings of the earth and their armies will assemble to make war against Jesus Christ. (Revelation 19:19)

The beast and the 10 horns will wage war against the Lamb, but the Lamb will overcome them. (Revelation 17:14)

The beast and the 10 horns will hate the harlot that rides the beast and they will burn her up with fire. (Revelation 17:16; 18:8,9,18; 19:3)

The Lord will slay him with the breath of His mouth, and bring him to an end by the appearance of His coming. (II Thessalonians 2:8)

The beast's dominion will be taken away, annihilated, and destroyed forever. (Daniel 7:26)

He will come to his end, and no one will help him. (Daniel 11:45)

The beast will go to destruction. (Revelation 17:8,11)

The beast and the false prophet will be seized and thrown alive into the lake of fire which burns with brimstone. (Revelation 19:20, Daniel 7:11)

The beast and the false prophet, and the devil, will be tormented in the lake of fire and brimstone day and night forever and ever. (Revelation 20:10)

The Sequence of Events Within Daniel's 70th Week

I. Daniel's 70th week is initiated by the antichrist making or confirming a covenant with Israel for seven years. Daniel 9:27

Israel's participation in this "covenant with death" (Isaiah 28:15, 18) may be "the" apostasy that is referred to in II Thessalonians 2:3.

During the **first half**, or first 3½ years, there will be false Christs, wars and rumors of wars, famines and death. All these are described by Jesus Christ as "the beginning of birth pangs." (Matthew 24:4-8; Mark 13:6-8; Luke 21:8-11a)

II. At the **midpoint**, all these things will happen:

1. The antichrist will break the covenant. He will enter the sanctuary/Temple/holy place, and will set up/commit the abomination of desolation. This abomination desolates/desecrates the Temple from the pinnacle/wing on down. (Daniel 9:27; Matthew 24:15; Mark 13:14)

2. When he breaks the covenant, and commits the abomination of desolation, the antichrist will reveal himself as the man of lawlessness, the man of destruction. He will oppose God, will exalt himself, will set himself up as god, and will demand that the world worship him as god. (Daniel 7:8,11a,20,25; Daniel 11:36-37; II Thessalonians 2:3-4; Revelation 13:6)

3. Some of the Jews, represented by the woman of Revelation 12, will flee to the wilderness where they will be divinely protected for the remaining 3½ years. (Revelation 12:6,14)

4. Invested with the power and authority of Satan, the antichrist will embark on a vicious, relentless persecution of the Jews. This reign of terror by the antichrist is called variously the Great Tribulation and the final period of the indignation, which will last 3½ years, also known as a time, times, and half a time, also known as 42 months, and also known as 1260 days. (Daniel 7:21,25; Daniel 11:36,44,45; 12:1, 7; Matthew 24:9,21-22; Mark 13:9,11-13,19-20; Revelation 12:13; Revelation 13:2)

III. Other activities that will occur during this **second half** of Daniel's 70th week:

1. The persecution of the Jews will result in the deaths of 2 out of 3 Jews worldwide, and possibly even 9 out of 10. (Zechariah 13:8-9; Isaiah 6:13)

2. Thwarted, however, in his attempt to reach the "woman" in the wilderness, the antichrist will expand his persecution to include Christians. (Revelation 12:11,15-17; Revelation 13:7)

3. The false prophet will require those who dwell on the earth to take the mark of the beast: one world economy. He will also require them to worship the beast/antichrist. All who refuse will be killed. (Revelation 13:12-17)

4. The hunting down and execution of Christians by the forces of the antichrist will be so successful that, for the sake of the elect, God will cut short the time of this Great Tribulation. (Matthew 24:22; Mark 13:20)

5. The sign of the end of the age: sun, moon, stars will go dark; the world will be plunged into darkness. (Matthew 24:29; Mark 13:24-25; Luke 21:25-26)

6. The sign of His coming: the darkness will be broken by the supernatural light, the shekinah glory, of the appearance of Jesus Christ in the heavens, Who will be visible to all. (Matthew 24:27, 30; Mark 13:26; Luke 21:27, 17:24; Revelation 1:7)

7. Jesus Christ will send forth His angels, who will collect His people from the four corners of creation; the dead in Christ will rise first, and then those who are alive on earth will be gathered up to be with Him. (Matthew 24:31; Mark 13:27; I Thessalonians 4:16-17)

8. The wrath of God (the Day of the Lord) will be poured out on the unbelievers (all those who remain on the earth). (Matthew 24:29-42; I Thessalonians 5:1-3; II Thessalonians 2:1-5; Revelation 6:17; 8-9; 14:17-20; 15:5-16:21)

SDG

Definitions

Daniel's 70th Week: a period of 7 years that will begin with the signing of a covenant brokered by the antichrist (although his identity as such will not yet be revealed) between Israel and other nations. Midway through this period of 7 years, the true identity of the antichrist will be revealed to the world and the Great Tribulation will begin. At the end of the 70th week, the Lord will return physically to the earth.

Great Tribulation: a time of intense persecution by the antichrist and his forces toward Jews first and then Christians. It will begin at the midpoint of Daniel's 70th week (meaning, 3½ years into it), and will last until some point near the end of the 70th week when the Lord will cut those days short.

Rapture: the "catching up" of all believers, whether dead or alive, to meet with Jesus Christ in the air, described in I Thessalonians 4:16-17 and in Matthew 24:30-31. It will not be secret; it will be visible to all, including those left behind on earth. It will occur at some time toward the end of the 70th week when the Lord cuts short the days of the Great Tribulation. As soon as every single believer is safely off the earth, the Lord will begin to pour out His wrath in the Day of the Lord.

Day of the Lord/Wrath of God: a period of time in which the Lord will punish, with no hope of restoration, unrepentant unbelievers on the earth. It will begin directly after the Lord cuts short the days of the Great Tribulation and gathers together or catches up His own in the rapture. This wrath of God in the Day of the Lord is described in Revelation as the trumpet and bowl judgments.

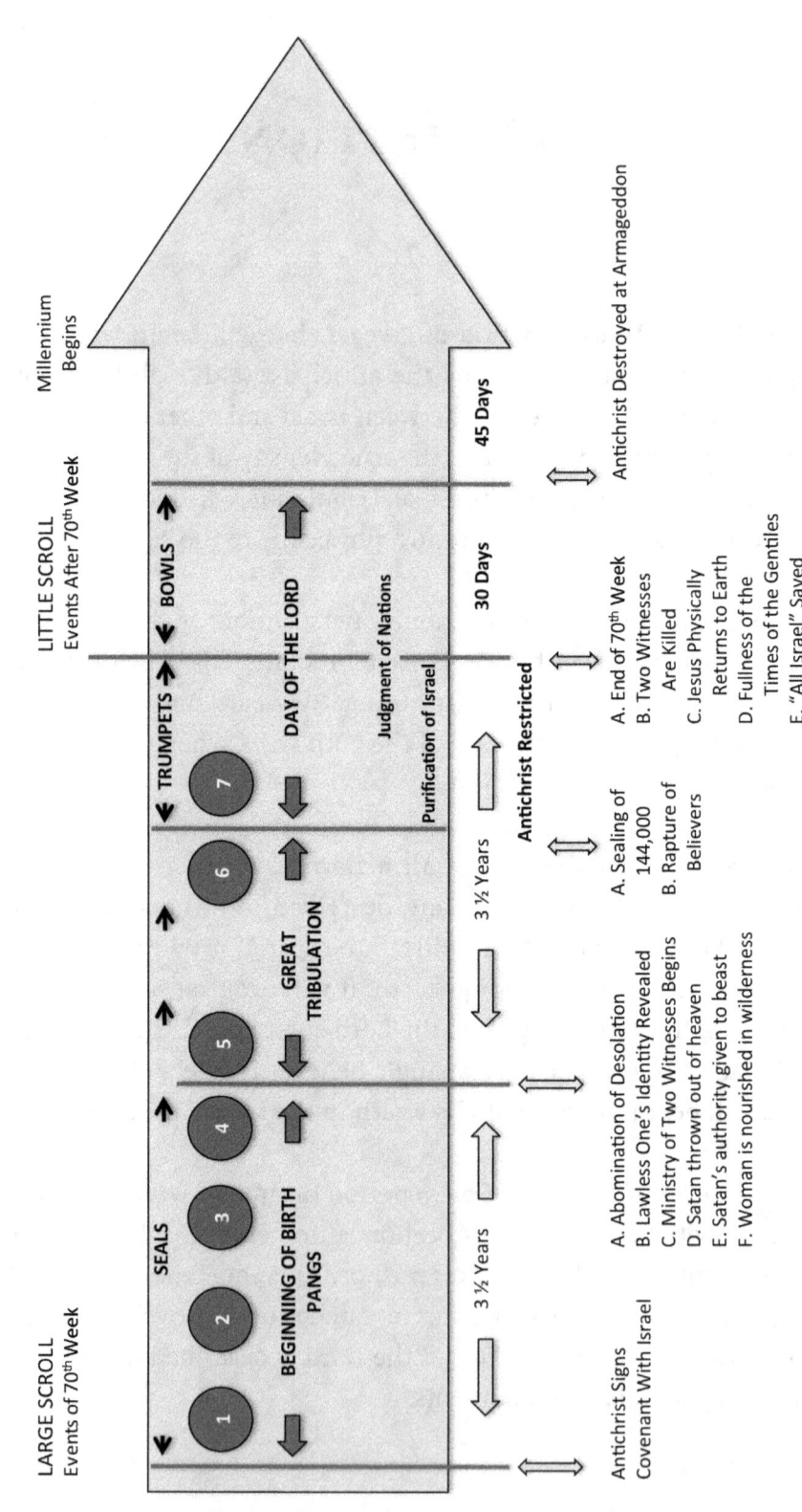

www.ingramcontent.com/pod-product-compliance
Lightning Source LLC
Chambersburg PA
CBHW071519080526
44588CB00011B/1493